FROM ANTICHRIST TO "I AM"

Harvest of Healing, LLC

Copyright 2022 by Harvest of Healing, LLC.

Published 2022.

Printed in the United States of America.

All rights reserved.

No portion of this book may be reproduced,
stored in a retrieval system, or transmitted in any form or by any means –
electronic, mechanical, photocopy, recording, scanning, or other – except for
brief quotations in critical reviews or articles, without the prior
written permission of the author.

ISBN 978-1-957077-13-0

Cover image: Copyright AlexKosev-Can Stock Photo Inc.

Publishing assistance by BookCrafters, Parker, Colorado.
www.bookcrafters.net

THE MIND SHOULD
NOT GUIDE THE SPIRIT,
THE SPIRIT SHOULD
GUIDE THE MIND

*This Book is dedicated to all
Current and future generations of Spiritual Royals
Who will continue to bring forth Ancient Customs
Resulting in the opportunity to live life in
The Way of I AM.*

Nuts and Bolts and a Few Loose Screws

The Big Picture...1

Why So Curious..3

Preprogramming..4

Run That By Me Again..6

Back In The Day...8

A Glance At History..10

Clearing Things Up...22

Is This The Way?...24

Past vs. Present..26

It's In The Blood...27

What Did You Say?...29

The Final Act..30

Closing...31

Terms...33

Topics..39

TOPIC INDEX

Adultery..43

Ancient Ways..46

Ark..48

Baptism...51

Blood..54

Born Again...57

Bread of Life...60

Breath/Breathe..63

Bride/Groom..65

Christ (and AntiChrist)......................................69

Communion...75

Dead, Death, Die, Died and Sleep, Slept.......78

First Adam/Last Adam......................................82

Glory..85

Heaven..87

I AM...90

Israel/Israelite...92

Jesus..96

Life..98

Mysteries..100

Passover..106

People Groups..108

Priest..113

Sabbath..116

Saints...120

Salvation..123

Sin..126

Solomon...133

Son of Man or Son of God................................135

Soul..138

Virgin Mary..142

Vow and Oath...144

Wheels..146

White Horse..150

Conclusion..153

NUTS AND BOLTS
AND A FEW LOOSE SCREWS

Isaiah 40:3: A voice of one crying out: Prepare the way of the Lord in the wilderness; make a straight highway for our God in the desert. (HCS)

I. THE BIG PICTURE

Scripture points to an Ancient past, long ago destroyed and in many cases, forgotten. Having the ability to verbalize the visual pictures I now see is challenging without producing an extended multiple volume series of books. How does one relay in understandable terms the nuts and bolts of what resulted in the great downfall of humanity? Fabricated stories seem to have filled in blanks where the vital points of instruction were missing. How does the order of life that will result in health and avoidance of disease and death translate into understandable words? Current life activities, social norms, family structures, and holiday celebrations have progressed in a way that has led mankind in the opposite direction from where they should be. What is the cause of this invisible yet captivating essence that is attracting people toward destruction?

We must discover what was involved in this Ancient past and bring it to the forefront of today. Second, to produce vitality in our physical life and in the cycles of nature, we must uncover who, by means of blood, we are and the role we are to play. Focus has been directed at skin color when the deeper identity lies beneath the surface written within the codes that flow through our veins. Carrying a title of "Child of God" (I Peter 1:5; Romans 8:19) is hidden within the blood, not within the registry of a religion of choice, or the result of a decision we make. The Topics that follow will shed some light on these points. There remains much to discover.

II. WHY SO CURIOUS?

Curiosity expands with a dose of determination. This combination, mixed with a dash of the "know that you know" that cannot be explained took me on a long and winding, mountainous and at times dangerous journey. In search of answers that did not exist in textbooks brought a conclusion that stepping into a traditional school was not where I would need to be. Experience was the most influential teacher and produced an education beyond what any textbook could provide. Patience, pain, insomnia, broken relationships and costly endeavors can all be courses in the subject of experience. Tenacity prevailed no matter what "home" work was assigned to me. Learning how to step out of a few premade boxes that had been erected around the mind and venturing into a few great unknowns was a must. Grasping the valuables and tossing out the contaminated proved an interesting journey. A few lessons on how to navigate with a new prescription to the lenses held within my internal eyeglasses developed a different perspective, a new way to look at old concepts. This new vision began to unfold the answers sought after. My body became an internal science lab and I had to learn how to respond to the messages it was giving me. Knowledge advanced into wisdom, wisdom to application.

III. PREPROGRAMMING

Childhood stories of Jonah literally being swallowed by a whale and surviving for three days in the amount of stomach acid just did not make sense! What about Lazarus? How did his physical body not begin the process of decay after having been dead for days? At some point the Laws of Nature have to be applied. No corpse would avoid the natural process of decay. So what happened? Then there is the story of the flood that wiped out the entire surface of the earth. I doubt today we witness an Ark being constructed as it was in the days of Noah; or people being hung on crosses; or Red Seas part that result in a pathway of dry land. What will continue to be experienced and has in recent years been experienced is the spiritual (good and bad) side of identical acts that took place long ago.

A walk through Scripture with a magnifying glass and a new perspective was my goal. Why the need for this new insight? Considering the past four hundred years of the common interpretations of Scripture and experiencing, or even just observing life in general, many things just didn't match up. The rules and stories told from pulpits for so many years didn't manifest for me, or for some of my acquaintances. Things were inside out, or upside down, compared to the rules and guidelines attached to religion. What was wrong? The Promises foretold of a blessed, prosperous, healthy life seemed lost in the pages called life. What happened? Knowing it could not be "God's will" for mankind to come to Earth to suffer deterioration, decay, disease or even extreme poverty, I began to search and pray for answers, for the Truth.

Attempting to unravel long told stories or theories that have become riddled with incorrect theories, gossip, or a whole lot of misdirected assumptions, are quite challenging to clear up. For those reasons, this book may seem complex and a bit challenging for many to follow. For those who have many years of a religious trained mindset, it will require setting aside some old patterns of thought.

Offering a new perspective is not often well received, is easily misunderstood and becomes tossed aside. I ask that the new pair of eyeglasses offered are accepted. Children of Israel, and I'm not referring to the nation, I am referring to God's title for a specific group of people, it's time to open the ears and hear.

Ezekiel 2:3-4: And he said unto me, Son of man, I send thee to the children of Israel, to a rebellious nation that hath rebelled against Me; they and their fathers have transgressed against Me, even unto this very day. For they are impudent children and stiffhearted, I do send thee unto them; and thou shalt say unto them. Thus saith the Lord God. (KJV)

IV. RUN THAT BY ME AGAIN

This book will cast new light on terms common to many. The Holy Bible contains metaphors that must be accompanied by skilled interpretation. In my search for answers, many references were consulted, along with good old common sense, a sprinkle of the Laws of Nature and a whole lot of prayer, resulting in a broader platform from which to work. Incorrect assumptions or interpretations can occur when a cherry-picking method through Scripture is made and not all relative information is taken into consideration. Not following the threads (or leads) from one verse, chapter or book to the next, the story line can become misleading. The story line flows smoothly when conclusions are not drawn prior to considering all that is involved.

Original Scripture text has gone through translations of varying types creating situations where multiple definitions for one subject may exist. Some Scripture needs a dose of clarification; some, a whole new interpretation. The Word remains, it is the eyes of understanding that will open.

An important component to a full interpretation of Scripture is considering the root meaning of a name, whether a person's name, city, country, mountain, etc. The root meaning of any given name reveals a backdrop or subject line for what the story is attempting to relay.

On my journey I discovered Sin was not what most believe. Sin, as it turns out, is a term used for the frequencies recorded in the blood cells; frequencies of harmful emotions, whether of one's own making or those of ancestors. Christ was not a person or something that is obtained by means of a prayer, but a term applied to the processes of Natural internal function of the physical body that purges harmful debris, including the Sin frequencies. This Christ transformation process was connected to Salvation, the rescue from the internal chaos the frequencies produce. It made sense. The search for the answers was paying off and the "Why?" was being pieced together. The Bible is instruction on how to achieve Abundant Life, it just has a little different flavor than once believed.

V. BACK IN THE DAY

Turning back the pages of time to a life lived long ago, there was a People Group that had a natural born ability of knowing; an instinct or even intuition that not every individual has. The kind of knowing that outsiders might think is peculiar, having an uncommon sort of way about them. This People Group were the kind that knew how to take an element from the Earth, such as an herb or branch, and use it to sooth a cold or flu; how to mend a wound or heal a broken heart; what to use to ward off snakes or treat snake bites. Adding a reference to Scripture through the means of a short poem, rhyme or charm to each antidote prepared, they were the ones consulted for healthcare and insight. There were no schools for this special kind of skill or knowing, it was in the blood, passed down from Mom and Pop, Grandma or Grandpa. I call them *Spiritual Royals*.

As time passed, ridicule, jealousy and bitter hearts crept into the community and the skills and customs were sold or traded to outsiders, resulting in the customs and skills becoming scattered, fragmented and contaminated, some possibly extinct. The knowledge of the customs and skills of this People Group gradually faded away, along with the genetic recipe that went with it.

Foreigners picked up the pieces and tried their hand at applying the skills but the results were never as precise or beneficial as that which came from the People Group with the natural born skills. Foreigners pressed in, determined to make things work, molding, sculpting, bending the rules, anything to replace that which the People Group had once mastered. Years rolled by and the counterfeit products and techniques began to grow in number, creating financial benefit for many involved, but never the result of longevity and vitality that once existed. Something was missing. With the takeover by Foreigners things progressed into a state of weakness, situations proved great loss was the result, rather than any gain for the benefit of people as a whole. The outcome was creating a cycle of disease, decay and eventually financial burden. What had happened? More important, how do the skills and customs resurrect into the hands of those who have the natural born ability to use them? How do we get to a Harvest of Healing?

VI. A GLANCE AT HISTORY

I was never one who would select a book on historical events over a book on health but a few historical events that were brought to my attention over the course of my quest to find answers to health issues became quite interesting. First, the year 1066 kept coming to my attention through various means so I grabbed the ipad and began a general search. Nothing really eye catching to me and as time went on another event related to those woven into the historical marker of 1066 would come to my attention. This is when I decided there was something more to these incidents that were catching my attention than what I was giving credit. These types of things are not always just a coincidence. To layout in my own words a very brief history line, I present what I came to discover:

William the Conqueror (aka William the Bastard as a result of his birth mother not being of royal blood) bullied his way to the power of the throne after the death of his father, keeping the rightful heir to the throne, William's Uncle, out of his birthright position as heir to the throne. William took his bullying tactics into Britain by means of a few battles, one battle being referenced as having "filled the river with blood." Battles were fought on horseback and most men of battle were expert archers back then so filling a waterway with blood would be quite easy. The bloody river detail caught my attention as I began to recall a verse in Revelation that speaks of a similar event:

Revelation 14:20: *Then the press was trampled outside the city, and blood flowed out of the press up to the horses bridles for about 180 miles. (HCS)*

There are several rivers in England that stretch to great lengths. In clips of History pertaining to William the Conqueror's battles, the following description appears: "the battle was long and bloody, the Saxons causing heavy Norwegian losses early on, before succumbing to the weight of the Viking attack. The Saxons were defeated and fled across the Ouse (river), many drowning in the flight..." (her.york.gov.uk). Given this written description and a few descriptions on documentaries by Smithsonian Channel, it gave rise to consider the verse in Revelation as being a reference to a battle of William the Conqueror, nearly six hundred years prior to King James writing the Holy Bible. Any further detail on the subject I will hand over to an expert Historian. The scene set here is an illegitimate son taking possession of the power of the throne and then takes that power and invades Britain. Remember these details as we move forward.

Advancing forward a few hundred years to the late 1500's to early 1600's, another set of interesting historical events took place. King James VI of Scotland became King James I of England and Ireland after the death of Queen Elizabeth I, spreading his influence over additional territory. Again, events from this time period were brought to my attention that caused me to take a more detailed look. King James just so happened to be King in three countries that were involved in the historical events known as the Witch Trials. King James seems to have had an influential role in the events that took place during this time, being King he had power to issue orders for the trial and murder of those who became categorized as participating in witchcraft. Knowing just a smidgen of information about the People Groups (clans) who occupied Scotland, Britain and Ireland the people in these areas would have been well known by one another and many most likely had same tribal roots if you track back far enough. At this point, it was beginning to look like King James, accompanied by a skeptical and likely very influential Catholic Church (esp. given Queen Isabella of Spain was an ancestor, amongst the twists of royal marriages, of King James), was on a mission to destroy a particular group of people who were once sought by church leaders and their congregation for healing remedies. Five hundred years prior, William the Conqueror came busting through the doors in this same territory of Britain. Being from Scotland, King James would have been familiar with the customs used for healing. Why would he take a position to destroy the persons who provided remedies for health? What was the underlying motive in action here? I was beginning to cast a suspicious eye upon King James. What could be behind such a plot? Scripture states the "love of money is the root of all evil."

Where would this feeling of suspicion be coming from? Certainly, I felt a deeper dig into the background of those put on trial and ultimately murdered for participating in witchcraft was a must. The fact remains, King James was right in the middle of an assignment set in place for mass murders.

I woke one morning with the name "Cornwall" in my mind. Cornwall? What is Cornwall? A quick search on the Internet and there she was, Cornwall, England. Then I remembered seeing "Cornwall" on my ancestry ledger. Seeking further answers, I purchased and read a book titled Cornish Witchcraft that proved to be a compilation of interviews conducted by a gentleman in the 1920's to 1930's. The book was published in Great Britain in 2016. The book contained a good collection of interviews had with then current residents in and around Cornwall, England. The interviewees were able to expand on the history of what actually took place during the time of the witch trials and they shared some interesting insight. There seems to have been a good number of what I will call Healers in and around the area for many years. These Healers were called upon when there was sickness whether in a person or livestock. They knew the herbs and plants to use and the prayers, which prior to invasion were called charms, to present to Heaven. A few of the charms shared in the book displayed as short rhythmic poems that included summon to the Heavens or God for His blessing. Prior to the use of the English language by the Healers, Gaelic would have likely been their native tongue. Some of the interviews suggested that the Healers would "speak in a way that was unknown" to some of the locals seeking a form of relief. This made another light go off in the memory bank of Biblical Scripture:

<u>I Corinthians 14:2</u>: *Pursue love and desire spiritual gifts, and above all that you may prophesy. For the person who speaks in another language is not speaking to men but to God, since no one understands him; however he speaks mysteries in the Spirit. (HCS)*

Is this a time for an "oh me!" or an "Amen!"? At this point I was tiptoeing rather than tromping through the remainder of the book. What else would I find?

Healers carried a title of Wise Women and Wise Men, not witches. (Scripture references holy women or holy men in various places.) The term "witch" had come from the organizers of the Witch Hunts and Trials. Everyone has heard of Wise Men if they know anything about the Christmas story so there's no need to share that bit of Scripture. The story of the life of Jesus is representative of Natural Healthcare and here we are unfolding acts that took place to murder the Healers of the 15th and 16th Century? I was beginning to wonder if this was a repeat of the Crucifixion of Christ!

Directing my view at Ireland and scanning Celtic Mythology of St. Patrick, it was discovered that portions (all in faint whispers of course) of the Celtic myth are repeated in the Holy Bible, with altered names and reference points. Example:

After dinner, the druid challenged Patrick to a duel of miracles on the plain before Tara. "What kind of miracle would you like me to do?" asked Patrick. "Let us call down snow on the land," the sorcerer replied. "I do not wish to do anything contrary to God and nature," said Patrick. "You are afraid you will fail," exclaimed Lucet Máel. "But I can do it." The druid uttered magic spells and called down snow from the sky so that it covered the whole plain up to the depth of a man's waist. "We have seen what harm you can do," said Patrick. "Now make the snow disappear." "I do not have the power to remove it until tomorrow," said Lucet Máel. Patrick then raised his hands and blessed the whole plain so that the snow disappeared in an instant. The crowd was amazed and cheered for the holy man. But the druids were very angry. Next, the druid invoked his evil gods and called down darkness on the whole land. The people were frightened and begged him to bring back the light, but he could not. But Patrick prayed to God and straightaway the sun shone forth and all the people shouted with joy. (Celtic Mythology by Philip Freeman)

Scripture gives a similar theme in various verses in Exodus 7, 8 and 9.

Exodus 7:10-12: So Moses and Aaron went in to Pharaoh and did just as the Lord had commanded. Aaron threw down his staff before Pharaoh and his officials, and it became a serpent. But then Pharaoh called the wise men and sorcerers – the magicians of Egypt, and they also did the same thing by their occult practices. Each one threw down his staff and it became a serpent. But Aaron's staff swallowed their staffs. (HCS)

Moving forward another leap to the 1930's and 1940's to the time of Hitler and Nazi Germany. Titles may be a little different in this movie but the results are the same, innocent people with a title of Jew being murdered. History does repeat it just takes on a different appearance.

This brings up yet another question, do I dare ask? Are the historian's terms of Anglo-Saxon and Celts one and the same as the terms Hebrew and Jew used by King James in Scripture? There seems to be a cyclical action in place here and by altering names it adds to the confusion, or the ability to keep information hidden.

I may be one of the first to confess, after having read the Holy Bible multiple times through its entirety and unknowingly being led to parts of history that appear to be screaming inside Scripture, King James wrote portions of the Holy Bible based on: 1) history that took place within his own familiar territory; and 2) customs and skills of the "witches" he ordered to be killed.

Being the King of England, King James would have been aware of the history of William the Conqueror and the tapestry that holds the visuals of the historical events that took place in 1066. King James likely had an elevated level of knowledge of the customs of the Wise Women and Wise Men, who were tried and killed on his watch. This all would open a door of opportunity for him or others in positions of power to take the customs, whether from personal knowledge or experience, recover any written text that would have been in the possession of the Healers and rewrite the knowledge into a new story.

Could King James have innocent blood on his hands and be guilty of having many innocent people, possibly from his own brotherhood, killed under a disguise of it all being called Witchcraft? Or was there a plan to overtake the skills of the Healers and form a means of profit making? To further cover up the dirty work being done, does he take the history of William the Conqueror (and possibly others), adds in information from any books of instruction plundered from those brutally murdered and writes a new book with a title of Holy Bible? Or is the Holy Bible in a code language King James wrote in hopes that one day someone would have the ability to piece it together and take back the Healing skills that had landed in the hands of the church? The Scripture frowns on "land" being "sold" (transferred). In this case, the "land" is the Healing Customs and Skills. (Leviticus 25:23). This transfer of property (Healing Customs) has resulted in a curse on the land (forms of healing). Herein lies an answer to why so many people who attend a church and seek out a benefit for recovery from the "healing ministry within" ultimately suffer and die. Does any of this lead to a connection to the "practitioners" many seek today; those inside the Medical Industry? It may be a good question to consider with a high percentage of people perishing at the hands of current day medicines. At this point, no one really knows all the answers. I can be sure of this much, there is something stinky in the woodpile here!

There's a high price to pay when innocent blood is shed and if this is truly what happened, it would be a partial explanation as to why similar events cycle around every few hundred years, from William the Conqueror to the Witch Trials and then to Hitler. Today we sit in the middle of an outbreak of COVID that has taken numerous lives although there is no way to track the roots of the lives lost. As far back as the story of Cain killing Abel, innocent blood cries out from the ground into the atmosphere and will keep making noise until someone with a God granted position of power steps up to put a stop to it. It may all sound farfetched until you dig into the Truth that lies deep beneath the root meanings of words used in Scripture. Was King James just hell-bent on destroying the customs he had grown up around out of pure shame or embarrassment, or for a little extra dough for the benefit of his castle and the church? This is all beginning to sound like a good theme for a movie!

Actions that take place on Earth by people who hold legally appointed positions of power (i.e., adopting laws; killing) record in the airwaves of the firmament, in the invisible. Those actions become the blueprint for spirit activity (good or bad) and remain there until someone with a birthright position of power identifies them and removes them. William the Conqueror set into place the ability for illegitimate people to rule over broad territories and masses of people through a position of a counterfeit ruling spiritual power. This blueprint was in the airwaves when King James comes on the scene, who then takes it on to begin killing the *Spiritual Royals*, the ones who held the birthright for working with the Spirit. This same pattern has trickled through the sands of time. Murder and deception has been in control of the airways for nearly one thousand years.

<u>II Peter 3:8</u>: *Dear friends, don't let this one thing escape you: With the Lord one day is like a thousand years, and a thousand years is like one day. (HCS)*

Reflecting on the verse in II Peter and the date of the birth of William the Conqueror 1027/28, are we approaching the end of a season where darkness has been in control of the airwaves above us? Are we on the brink of seeing a shift and change? Is this what is referenced in Scripture as "End Times," the end of what started nearly one thousand years ago that left murder and deception imprints in the airwaves? The year 1066 marks illegitimate takeover with the Witch Trials synching things up with the death of those called Wise Women and Wise Men (*Spiritual Royals*). Will 2066 be a year we witness the full recovery of the Ancient Customs? I would not be surprised if this proves to be so. At whatever year the coming shift takes place, it will ignite the prophesy of the Saints (those who "hear" directly from deities) ruling with the Lord for one thousand years. The tables turn and face a new direction; the airwaves will no longer contain the murder and deception imprints! The Harvest of Healing will arrive! Thus sayeth the Lord!

Parts of my journey continued, as you will see in the Topics I share herein, and parts I had to lay aside just out of the deep sorrow I felt in my heart. It was one of those "hope it isn't" situations yet you "know that it is." At times the thought of Daniel raced through my mind, how he gasped and fell weak for days at the visions he had of what would take place.

Daniel 8:27: And I Daniel fainted, and was sick certain days; afterward I rose up, and did the king's business; and I was astonished at the vision, but none understood it. (KJV)

His visions were of events being lived out today; and the events our parents or grandparents lived through. It is horrifying, even breathtaking and to a degree traumatizing to realize the level of contamination that has developed. God's wrath, at this point, seems minor compared to what is deserved. It causes me to shake my head and proclaim "it is no wonder!"

Genesis 4:2-12: Then she also gave birth to his brother Abel. Now Abel became a shepherd of flocks (Spirit work), but Cain worked the ground (Earth work). In the course of time Cain presented some of the land's produce as an offering to the Lord. And Abel also presented an offering – some of the firstborn of his flock and their fat portions. The Lord had regard for Abel and his offering but He did not have regard for Cain and his offering, Cain was furious, and he looked despondent. Then the Lord said to Cain, "Why are you furious?

And why do you look despondent. If you do what is right, won't you be accepted? But if you do not do what is right, sin is crouching at the door. Its desire is for you, but you must rule over it." Cain said to his brother Abel, "Let's go out to the field." And while they were in the field, Cain attacked his brother Abel and killed him. Then the Lord said to Cain, "Where is your brother, Abel?" "I don't know he replied, Am I my brother's guardian?" Then He said, "What have you done? **Your brother's blood cries out to Me** *from the ground! So now you are cursed, alienated from the ground that opened its mouth to receive your brother's blood you have shed. If you work the ground, it will never again give you its yield. You will be a restless wanderer on the earth. (KJV) (Inserts added; Emphasis added)*

Same story that has always been heard but with a new face it is telling us about anger and jealousy fueling a deadly situation between one who has the Spiritual Gifts (Abel) and one who does not (Cain, worker of the earth). The jealousy and anger triggered the spilling of innocent blood that led to a curse. Today, the curse must be reversed if the cycle is to cease.

Threads: Blood; Bride/Groom

VII. CLEARING THINGS UP

Throughout Scripture specific People Groups or Tribes were being addressed. What is required or good for one People Group or Tribe may not be so for another. Blending all the instructions together can result in confusion and seeming contradiction. With what I share, some of those gray areas will become less convoluted.

The Holy Bible can be considered an owner's manual for the physical body. A set of instructions for the health, well-being and vitality human life was designed to experience. The life journey on Earth is to be enjoyed, and just like with automobiles, there are specific instructions given to the various models of humans. Not all models are the same. An individual may be given a physical body with specific maintenance instructions they do not necessarily want or desire, but in order to maintain a properly running Earth suit (vehicle), the owner's manual must be obeyed.

The power and creativity of what took place to form the living environment we call Earth, the universal display of magnificence, that some call an act of the Universe, should not be ignored. Sure there are technical Science terms for how the Earth was formed but this book focuses on the invisible energy force(s) behind the scenes that are available for use within our physical body, without all the fancy words. The words God and Universe are closely knit together and in certain circumstances become interchangeable. Conversations become divided by technicalities when many times the conversation is reflective of the same point of interest. Science has terms and religion has terms yet there are places that a shaking of the hands would benefit all.

To be clear, God is still God; He is, and was, our Creator; He is powerful and deserves far more than any human can offer. It is not my job to cast upon the audience a pointing finger, a scolding frown or criminal sentence. My job is to present information with the Spirit blessing upon it and at whatever level it is received is the level it needs to be for that one person at this given time.

VIII. IS THIS THE WAY?

<u>John 14:6</u>: *Jesus saith unto him, I am the way, the truth, and the life; no man cometh unto the Father, but by me. (KJV)*

"The Way", referenced in John 14:6, is different than what has been believed. People have been enslaved, locked into a specific mindset. Today, there are billions who profess a belief in God. If "the Way" was being properly applied today, wouldn't it make sense that life on Earth would look much better than it currently does? It appears a mass exodus from the current mindsets must happen in order for people to be free from the cycle of decay and disease, not only for the benefit of humanity, but also for the health and benefit of the Earth herself.

There is an exchange between Heaven and a People Group, referred to as Royals in Scripture (*Spiritual Royals*) that must take place in order for current and future generations to live healthy. *Heaven Energy* has been closed off. The Heaven exchange requires: 1) Being granted permission through genetics to participate; 2) Effort and time to learn how *Heaven Energy* operates.

In years past, an individual may have been connected to something "out there" but it is unlikely its entirety was the

Heaven Energy I am referring to which is genuine, no counterfeits. There is no reaping a benefit of *Heaven Energy* when the correct combination to access it is not applied to the lock that holds it secure. That combination secret is held in genetics. No union between *Heaven Energy* and any person or group has existed for hundreds of years.

IX. PAST vs. PRESENT

What is printed on the pages of this book does not take away the value of Holy Scripture. The interpretation of past events for application in the current day in time is what is presented. Many of the recorded events that took place long ago are unfolding now through a means of various spirit (invisible) activities, they just come with a different flavor or color the second time around. When release of a specific intention occurs under the authority of a person in a position of power, that intention (aka spirit influence) will remain until it is properly removed. It is like a recipe that calls for adding a flavoring, you taste and know it is there but don't see it.

X. IT'S IN THE BLOOD

Human blood contains frequencies. The frequencies are not always heard but the result of the frequency produces a wave of energy one would emit. Animals sense their surroundings through frequencies.

Laboratory blood tests reveal what an individual has eaten, how well they exercise, or not, what diseases or challenges the ancestors had. These are the standard blood test results received from your doctor's office. What have not been tested, to my knowledge, are the frequencies recorded in blood. I call these frequencies imprints. These frequencies, if contaminated, are what can later develop into disease. How do the frequencies get there? And more importantly, what can be done to erase the harmful ones?

The blood acts as the DVD; the brain is the TV screen on which the recordings play; and the Soul plays the music (mood) for the show. These recordings can be televised during the day and are expressed through emotions or physical reactions, or they can play during sleep in the form of a dream.

Blood frequencies can also contain an unusual message;

a message put in place by God. A unique and different way of identifying people, a way that man has yet to discover. The inner workings of the physical body tell a different story, one in particular related to a genetic code that reflects a status of a *Spiritual Royal*.

XI. WHAT DID YOU SAY?

It cannot be expressed enough, especially to those who have been brought up in a religious faith, how unreal, unbelievable, shocking, or even disturbing some of the information printed herein will seem. Disbelief and tears rushed over me, but time and time again what was thought as "just can't be" was confirmed as Truth, never thinking my search for the meaning of Sin would lead to what it has. This book is intended to guide mankind to the true Salvation and Eternal Life heard of for so long. The Salvation and Eternal Life experienced by some of our ancestors.

XII. THE FINAL ACT

Give this information time to simmer; ask God for insight from Heaven. One page, or even one Topic will not reveal the entirety of the message. It takes time to weave a fabric from mere threads. This is not a one afternoon read. Parts may be uplifting, a sign of relief or even troubling. With that, please be seated and buckle up, the ride can be rough at times. Hang in there!

<u>Romans 8:19</u>: *The creation waits in eager expectation for the children of God to be revealed. (KJV)*

XIII. CLOSING

Believing the information shared, or not, is up to the recipient. No position is taken to persuade anyone for any reason. Sharing what I have come to know, with a hope that someday a Scientist or Biologist will become aware of the information and begin to discover a means for tangible evidence to what is shared. People desire proof. I do not own a laboratory and I am not a Scientist or Biologist. What I am is a messenger.

TERMS

Bride: Those who seek with earnest after the Ancient Ways. They long for the return of Ancient Customs and Skills that influence their *E-motional* heart and physical body.

Bridegroom: The Ancient Customs that were lost hundreds of years ago.

E-motion. Electrical conduction within the body causing a motion that interferes with the health and vitality of the Wheels (Chakras). The 'E' is separated to emphasize the electrical response to an emotion.

Earth Dust is a term selected to identify persons who are genetically predestined to be the workers, gathers and providers for the worldly life. These people are great business owners, excellent employees and connect to their job or career. They may or may not accept or understand the concepts of Heaven Energy. They lean toward the need for tangible evidence.

Heaven Energy is a term selected to reference the invisible, powerful, potentially life altering force(s) that come from the Heavens or Firmament and Universe that have an influence on the atmosphere in which we live and the physical body we occupy.

Jesus is representative of the use of Natural Healthcare and Wellness. Natural Healthcare and Wellness is used during and after the Christ transformation process and will produce life and vitality for the physical body.

People Groups/Tribes reference a classification of people that lived many years ago and shared a common ancestor root. Some of the members of this group carried a genetic code for operating in Spiritual Gifts and the Ancient Customs that accompanied the activity of those Gifts.

Spiritual Royal is the term selected to describe the genetic inheritance of or genetic advancement toward Spiritual Gifts. The evidence of the Spiritual Gifts will unfold through what is called the "royal priesthood" in Scripture. Spiritual Royals have the Star Dust in their blood and are identified by specific features described in the Topics.

Star Dust is a term selected to reference the people who hold within their genetic codes an imprint of Heaven Energy (Spirit) that is to be used not only for their own benefit but also for the benefit of those around them. Star Dust people do not connect well to a worldly focused job or career unless it has a connection to Heaven Energy work. Abundance of Star Dust results in a *Spiritual Royal*.

Threads are noted at the end of each Topic to direct

the reader to relative Topics. One Topic will connect to one or multiple Topics and should all be taken into consideration, though not in any given order, before drawing concrete conclusions.

TOPICS

Topics are the subjects; the contents of each Topic are in a form of Reference Guide rather than a storyline. The Topics include common expressions used in connection with God or other sources of an invisible (to the naked eye) influence. A Topic may begin with a definition the writer felt necessary to bring detail to the attention of the reader followed by Scripture references. With many Topics that need a revelatory light directed at them, caution was taken and a Topic may provide more description than necessary at times with the hope that the information is easily grasped.

There will be Topics that cause question, a few doubts, a dash of sorrow, a measure of fear, and flat out disbelief. I get it. I was there too. Some information is a bit hard to process. When you learn to apply Scripture one specific way for many years it is challenging for the brain to take on a new line of thought. The ruts created by the years of travel along the same path want to dominate. Then new insight comes to you, that you question, but after some sifting begins to make more sense than the conclusions to stories heard for so long. The pieces that were missing, upside down or backwards all those years, in all those stories or sermons or Bible studies, begin to take shape. A splash of joy will come forth when the reader recognizes the path once traveled by many of our ancestors, and the New Life path that lies ahead of us.

Learning to read the pictures displayed through life events is important. They often contain nuggets of insight needed at that particular time. A deeper dive into the terminology and definitions shared in each Topic unfold some of the mysteries of old and answers to what is being lived out today.

Note: Topics are listed in alphabetical order, not by any order of importance.

ADULTERY

<u>Adultery</u>: Consensual sexual intercourse between a married person and a person other than the spouse. Violation of the marriage-bed; carnal connection of a married person with any other than the lawful spouse. All manner of lewdness or unchastity in act or thought.

<u>Matthew 15:19</u>: For out of the heart proceed evil thoughts, murders, adulteries, fornication, thefts, false witness, blasphemies; these are the things which defile a man; but to eat with unwashed hands defileth not a man. (KJV)

Two categories of adultery exist; physical and E-motional. It's obvious what physical adultery involves. E-motional adultery is more complex, easily hidden.

When an individual connects with another it can be through interests or *E-motions*, it does not have to be through physical touch. The electrical conduction produced by what is called <u>emotions</u> causes a motion (or activity) within the physical body that will affect the electrical centers (Wheels) that run along the spine.

When an individual becomes *E-motionally* attached to another person, it can quickly become a form of adultery. Husband and wife are to be connected through values and goals; *E-motions* connect with each other; one can pick up on what the other thinks, likes or dislikes. When a third party comes into the picture and connects in similar or like ways to one of the spouses, that is adultery. Young children can have an *E-motional* connection to their parent/s but once they reach a certain age, usually in their teens, a gradual weaning from the parent/s begins. The child is taught how to become independent in order for him/her to be connected to a future spouse.

What about being *E-motionally* bonded to an organization? Yes, this can develop into adultery. The individual *E-motionally* bonded to the organization gives their time, energy, commitment to the organization, and eventually the other individuals within that organization. The spouse takes second chair. Adultery abounds. These third-party connections will destroy a marriage and a family.

A job should be just that, a job; employees need to be employees, not children or best friends. Limiting social interaction; not sharing personal information is a way to remain at arms-length from others. Social media has swung the doors wide open for every opportunity to share everything about your life and personal matters to many around the world. This creates ample opportunity for third-party interruptions in marriage or committed relationships. A polygamy type lifestyle begins on strictly the *E-motional* connections; intimate activity, minus physical touch, abounds via *E-motional* connection to several people.

Remember the story of the Samaritan woman Jesus encountered at the well? Jesus tells her that he knew she had had five husbands. Considering divorce was uncommon back then, it is unlikely the woman had the experience of five marriages. One had to have specific convincing evidence for the granting of a divorce. The Samaritan woman had not physically married five times she *E-motionally* bonded with five different men. A water well represents deep, buried emotions.

Avoiding potential *E-motional* connections may be one reason why families remained somewhat isolated from others in the past. Tribes stuck with their own Tribe.

This all raises the question of homosexuality referenced in Scripture. Does an *E-motional* adultery shed a different perspective on the term homosexual? The plot thickens.

ANCIENT WAYS

Ancient: A flag, banner, or standard; an ensign; especially the flag or streamer of a ship. The bearer of a flag; a standard-bearer. Having had an existence for many years. Old in wisdom and experience.

Daniel 7:9, 13, 22: I beheld till the thrones were cast down, and the Ancient of days did sit, whose garment was white as snow, and the hair of his head like the pure wool; his throne was like the fiery flame, and his wheels as burning fire. v. 13: I saw in the night visions, and behold, one like the Son of man came with the clouds of heaven, and came to the Ancient of days, and they brought him near before him. v. 22: Until the Ancient of days came, and judgment was given to the saints of the most High; and the time came that the saints possessed the kingdom. (KJV)

Proverbs 22:28: Remove not the ancient landmark, which thy fathers have set. (KJV)

Isaiah 61:4: And they shall build the old wastes, they shall raise up the former desolations, and they shall repair the waste cities, the desolations of many generations. (KJV)

I Peter 3:5: For after this manner, in the old time the holy women also, who trusted in God, adorned themselves, being in subjection unto their own husbands. (KJV)

Scripture references the term Ancient with: landmarks, cities, ruins, paths and highways. Ancient is referencing customs that existed several hundred, quite possibly thousands of years ago. Ancient of days is a reference to a period of time in history that was governed by a power directly from God (*Heaven Energy*). The Ancient information and way of living is what will be resurrected, and used again.

Holy women reference an unwavering Spiritual knowledge; a knowledge and wisdom not influenced by logical thoughts. They were the real deal when it came to being a Bride of Christ. The ways of the *Heaven Energy* was their husband that they held near and dear to their heart. Hundreds of years ago women or men with this unwavering way about them were known as Wise Women or Wise Men.

Threads: Bride; People Groups

ARK

Ark: A place of refuge. A chest containing the Ten Commandments; boat built by Noah for survival during the flood.

Uzzah: To shine. Give or be light.

Nachon: Intuitive knowledge; near accidental skill; snake by means of unpure mental processing.

I Peter 3:20: Which sometime were disobedient, when once the longsuffering of God waited in the days of Noah, while the ark was a preparing, wherein few that is eight souls were saved by water. (KJV)

II Samuel 6:6-7: When they came to Nachon's threshing floor, Uzzah reached out to the ark of God and took hold of it because the oxen had stumbled. Then the Lord's anger burned against Uzzah, and God struck him dead on the spot for his irreverence, and he died there next to the ark of God. (HCS)

Stories of "Ark," being that of Noah or of the Covenant, reference a People Group who know how to keep the Soul in a healthy condition and the catastrophes that can happen when mental processing takes over. The stories in Scripture expose detail, when root meanings of the various symbols are applied, of what is required in order to keep the Soul free of clutter and carry Heaven Energy.

As described by the events leading up to Uzzah's death in II Samuel 6, alterations in the guidelines for carrying or using Heaven Energy can be deadly.

Uzzah appears to have acted by means of mental processing versus intuition that resulted in a catastrophe. He had a gift of intuition but corrupted it by the process of logical thinking, likely triggered by an E-motion or influence of one in a position of authority. This same logical thought process is what resulted in Adam and Eve being escorted out of their abundant and prosperous lifestyle. Death can represent the loss of the intuitive gift.

The story of Noah reflects a total of eight Souls that escaped the flood, all relatives of Noah. Why were there only eight; and why the reference to their Soul?

To qualify for carrying the Ark level of Heaven Energy, the Soul must be cleansed of all E-motional Soul debris. Water (fluids) assist in flushing out present E-motions and prerecorded E-motions. The condition of the Soul is a qualifying factor before being granted permission to work with the Ark kind of Heaven Energy. Few qualify.

A flood represents being overcome by E-motions

connected to life circumstances. *E-motions* that lie beneath the surface and go unattended will eventually result in disease. Whether you survive that disease is one issue, but the more important issue is, who will escape the flood of *E-motions?* Appears Noah's family knew how to clean up the *E-motional* debris.

Threads: Baptism; Christ; Priest; Soul

BAPTISM

<u>Baptism</u>: An initiatory experience, act or effort.

<u>Matthew 3:1</u>: *In those days came John the Baptist, preaching in the wilderness of Judea, and saying, Repent ye, for the kingdom of heaven is at hand. (KJV)*

<u>Luke 7:33</u>: *For John the Baptist came neither eating bread nor drinking wine; and ye say, He hath a devil. (KJV)*

<u>Baptism</u> (<u>author's definition</u>): The initial efforts made to submerge yourself into the actions(s) necessary to cleanse the *E-motional* injuries personally experienced or passed on from ancestors. Baptism references the experience of the cleansing process that must take place in order to move on to being escorted or accompanied by the Holy Spirit component of *Heaven Energy*.

E-motional injuries record in cells. Water/fluid in the body retain the frequencies given off by an elevated or lingering *E-motion*; the adrenal glands secrete a chemical response and when left in the system the *E-motion(s)* and chemicals get stuck in the cells. With the numerous references to blood in Scripture, I suggest the imprints of the *E-motions* reside in the blood cells. The blood being imprinted with *E-motions* gives rise to the imprints passing through the bloodline.

John the Baptist, a cousin of Jesus, was born a few months prior to Jesus, referencing the Baptism process must take place prior to acquiring the Natural Healthcare cycles taking place within the body. The process represented by John the Baptist takes a given period of time as indicated by the difference in age of John the Baptist and Jesus, and leads to a state of healthy living, accompanied by the Holy Spirit.

In Matthew 3, wilderness reflects having no beneficial strategy when in situations that are challenging; Judea is the bloodline of Judah (aka specific People Group); and Kingdom of Heaven references the state of physical comfort or bliss that will take precedence within the body.

Luke 7 tells us John the Baptist is a Spiritual process that cleans *E-motional* imprints (from the body) and must be completed prior to being granted the power that descends from Holy Spirit (*Heaven Energy*). This level of power does not exist on Earth without being funneled through an individual who has been granted the ability to contain and distribute it. After the necessary cleansing processes, an individual can become a Medium or Mediator for the *Heaven Energy* to come through to Earth. A type of circuit regulator or place of exchange for the electrical charge to pass through, otherwise the voltage would be deadly. The status of the internal function of the body and electrical charge within the cells is key.

This process was not a belief amongst the common masses who must have been challenged to perceive the concept displayed. They place the John the Baptist process in a category of being from "the devil." It can be challenging to comprehend what has taken place when activity only exists in the unseen, inside the body. Scripture attaches names and faces to actions or events that exist in the realm of the invisible.

Threads: Ark; Blood

BLOOD

<u>B</u>lood: The fluid consisting of plasma, blood cells and platelets that is circulated by the heart through the vertebrate vascular system, carrying oxygen and nutrients to and waste materials away from all body tissues.

<u>S</u>aul: Request, petition, desire or ask.

<u>J</u>onathan: Give or bestow; to be "gifted" something with an authority attached.

<u>D</u>avid: Beloved one; intimately connected; praise, hand. Illness or disease and flow of fluids; ink.

<u>Proverbs 4:23</u>: Keep thy heart with all diligence for out of it are the issues of life. (KJV)

<u>Genesis 4:10</u>: And he said, What hast thou done? The voice of thy brother's blood crieth unto me from the ground. (KJV)

<u>I Samuel 18:1</u>: And it came to pass that when he had made an end to his speaking unto Saul that the soul of Jonathan was knit with the soul of David and Jonathan loved him as his own soul. (KJV)

<u>Luke 11:9</u>: And I say unto you, Ask and it shall be given you;

seek, and ye shall find; knock, and it shall be opened unto you. (KJV)

Blood does not move without the function of the heart organ; *E-motions* circulate by the function of the heart as well. Blood carries more information than what man has the current capability to test. Patterns and habits of ancestors can be seen in a standard blood test result labeled as inherited disease. Yet there is a form of information from ancestors that has not come to the table. The life experiences, continual thoughts that swirled about their minds, the persistent *E-motional* experiences they had, and environments in which they lived all record in the blood as frequencies (imprints). The harmful frequencies that later develop into disease, alcoholism, mental illness, etc., is what Scripture calls "sin." There is a process by which these harmful frequencies can be eliminated. The process takes time and effort, but it can be done.

When an individual goes through their physical life attempting to ward off the various frequency imprints in the blood that have developed into disease, it results in a walk through a Valley of the Shadow of Death, a hellish experience. Some may survive disease others may suffer horribly to their death. To escape the pattern of disease passed down through the generations, the harmful imprints must be erased. Erasing the harmful imprints allows the individual to live in a state of freedom, needing only to address their own periodic setbacks.

The individual can be who they were created to be, not the repeated *E-motions* or actions of their ancestors nor become trapped in their own traumatizing experiences.

David's name alone seems to describe the imprints held in the blood that result in disease; and the bloodline of those who have *Star Dust* in their blood that allows access to the *Heaven Energy* gifts. David is an ancestor of Jesus.

Interpretation of 1 Samuel 18:1: The beloved, Royals (Judah bloodline), have a mark (ink) in the blood (flow of fluids); they are bestowed a gift (skill) upon the completion of their requests. The requests are what an individual must present to God for the process to begin that relieves the Soul of the influences of harmful imprints and initiates a Spiritual Gift. Jonathan (gift) begins an ongoing exchange with David (Beloved Royal). The exchange (love) between Jonathan and David speaks of a group of Judah Spiritual Royals (who have the *Star Dust*) coming to a position of exchange with the *Heaven Energy*. This exchange is named Love, the acts of giving and receiving. *Heaven Energy* waits for a request from an individual, just like the court system requires a Petition to be filed to initiate a case.

Threads: People Groups; Soul

BORN AGAIN

<u>B</u>orn: Having gone through a birth process; to come forth.

<u>B</u>irth: The emergence of something new; the start of new life.

<u>A</u>gain: To repeat (*what was done in the flesh*); double.

<u>I Peter 1:3-4, 23</u>: Blessed by the God and Father of our Lord Jesus Christ, which according to his abundant mercy hath begotten us again unto a lively hope by the resurrection of Jesus Christ from the dead. To an inheritance incorruptible and undefiled, and that fadeth not away, reserved in heaven for you. <u>v. 23</u>: Being born again, not of corruptible seed, but of incorruptible, by the word of God, which liveth and abideth forever. (KJV)

<u>John 3:3</u>: Verily, verily, I say unto thee, Except a man be born again he cannot see the kingdom of God. (KJV)

<u>I John 3:9 and 5:18</u>: Everyone who has been born of God does not sin, because His seed remains in him; he is not able to sin, because he has been born of God. <u>5:18</u>: We know that everyone who has been born of God does not sin, but the One who is born of God keeps him, and the evil one does not touch him. (HCS)

Everyone reading this page has experienced a physical birthing process. There is a mirrored image of that process that takes place in the Spirit. I'm certain there is no need to expand on the process required for the conception and birth of a child so using your skill of recollection, let's walk through the process for Spiritual birth.

First, God (through a means of *Heaven Energy*) is the initiator of the act to bring about conception. An individual can present a request but God ultimately decides who the recipient of His incorruptible seed will be. If God does not initiate the process, there will be no Spiritual birth. Once God has initiated the process, it takes a specified period of time for the Spiritual Life to develop and be brought forth, just like in a natural pregnancy. What is this process?

Harmful *E-motional* frequencies, which are described in detail in some of the other Topics, keep an individual bound to that particular *E-motional* experience. The harmful frequencies could be the reference to "evil", once they are cleared out, the "God" (*Heaven Energy*) occupies the cells and evil can no longer get in. These *E-motional* frequencies cause friction to the natural electrical function of the body (*See Topic*, Wheels) that through time hinders the function of the organs and glands. These harmful frequencies must be erased to allow birth of the Spiritual Life otherwise the individual lives in the corruptible, anchored to a flesh life of decay and disease. Once the Spiritual birthing process is complete, the individual is free from Sin and will never return to it. (I John 3:9 and 5:18)

Threads: Ancient Ways; Christ; Sin

BREAD OF LIFE

<u>Bread</u>: Staple food; sustenance; necessary for sustaining life.

<u>John 6:31, 33, 35, 51</u>: *Our fathers did eat manna in the desert; as it is written, He gave them bread from heaven to eat. <u>v. 33</u>: For the bread of God is he which cometh down from heaven, and giveth life unto the world. <u>v. 35</u>: And Jesus said unto them, I am the bread of life; he that cometh to me shall never hunger; and he that believeth on me shall never thirst. <u>v. 51</u>: I am the living bread which came down from heaven; if any man eat of this bread, he shall live for ever; and the bread that I will give is my flesh, which I will give for the life of the world. (KJV)*

Eating bread is a physical activity that has an identical twin action and result in the Spiritual. Spiritual bread is invisible yet vital for health of the Soul and Spirit Life.

The verses in John speak of ancestors (fathers) that had the ability to receive this Heaven Bread even though they were living in some unsupported and challenging times. Heaven Bread is the *Heaven Energy* produced by the planets and stars. This *Heaven Energy* is a source of electrical fuel for the human body. Have you ever felt more sensitive emotionally on a full moon or new moon day?

When planets align in the ways planets do their dance, it gives off a source of energy. This energy moves the tides in the ocean and can certainly move you internally.

Then there is a reference to God Bread; a more specific source of Spirit nourishment than Heaven Bread. God Bread is the personal interaction with God versus a general knowing and recognizing God. This is when the electrical charge at a "God" level takes over your cells. You are now a product of "incorruptible seed".

Then Jesus comes on the scene as Life Bread, how to maintain the natural processes of the physical body and keep the cells healthy. I AM is the Living Bread, the *Heaven Energy* continually delivered directly to an individual that provides the healthy physical body function for the eternal Spirit within them. When the physical body takes in (eats) this *Heaven Energy* (Heaven Bread, God Bread and Life Bread), the Spirit within that person becomes eternal. In order for the flesh to maintain vitality that comes from *Heaven Energy*, things in/of the world will need to be adjusted or set aside. What would this look like? Some things that can result in harm to the level of *Heaven Energy* contained within the body include routine invasive health exams or tests; preserved or processed foods, high sodium intake, refined sugars and caffeine, all are common and difficult to avoid especially when eating away from home; and textbook logic that overrides Spirit wisdom. "Life charged" foods are not compatible with the standard food pyramid. There are many foods that have a stamp of approval for consumption and sold for their seeming benefit that actually deplete the electrical charge within a cell or cause an unidentified stress within the body.

Threads: Ancient Ways; Breath/Breathe

BREATH/BREATHE

Genesis 2:7: And the Lord God formed man of the dust of the ground, and breathed into his nostrils the breath of life; and man became a living soul. (KJV)

Psalm 150:6: Let everything that hath breath praise the Lord. Praise ye the Lord. (KJV)

Ezekiel 37:9: Then said he unto me, Prophesy unto the wind, prophesy, son of man, and say to the wind, Thus saith the Lord God, Come from the four winds, O breath, and breathe upon the slain, that they may live. (KJV)

A person must learn how to properly breathe. Breath is the life.

Shallow breathing is not sufficient for the proper function and health of organs; the muscles tense up; lungs cannot detox properly. A new born baby displays the healthy breathing technique. Your belly must expand, filling the chest cavity and abdomen of your body with air in through the nose, from the belly, lungs, and air reaching the neck, then let the air out through the mouth. This process aids detoxification, moves the muscles, and assists blood circulation. It is a basic life practice. Want to add life to your Soul? Breathe as God instructed.

Is Scripture suggesting that when proper breathing is not maintained the Soul could become classified as dead? In order for the Soul to be "living" (energized), there must be the God style of breathing, according to Genesis 2. Interestingly, Scripture does not prescribe any specific breath being given to other living creatures. Humans seem to be the only living species given a specific breath technique. Do other creatures automatically maintain their status with their breath and humans can alter their status with the breath?

God is invisible energy (Heaven Energy) that travels with/by means of the breath through the body maintaining electrical function within the body. Need a visual: Wind Generators.

No doubt the COVID pandemic sent ripples of various affects throughout the world. From loss of physical life, to loss of personal contact with loved ones, to restricting practically every freedom humanity once knew. Could COVID be a shout out from Heaven that proper breathing has been lost and Souls are perishing? Becoming familiar with how to read the signs around us is important.

Breath is the Praise, and has the ability to assist in recharge of a Soul back unto life.

Threads: Bread of Life; Soul

BRIDE/GROOM

<u>Bride</u>: One who has recently married; lace making or needlework; a thread or loop that joins parts of a pattern.

<u>Bride</u> (author's definition): Those who seek with earnest after the Ancient Customs. They long for the return of Ancient Customs and skills that influence their *E-motional* heart and physical body. This Bride would be classified as a *Spiritual Royal*.

<u>Groom</u>: One who has recently married; <u>One of several officers in an English royal household</u>.

<u>Bridegroom</u> (author's definition): The Ancient Customs lost hundreds of years ago that invite and serve the presence of what I call Ancient Customs Holy Spirit Fire. Some of those Customs include Natural Healthcare and Wellness (Jesus) and the Christ transformation process (Topic: Christ).

The Book of Song of Solomon describes how the *Spiritual Royal* Bride seeks and hungers for the Bridegroom of Natural Healthcare and Wellness Customs.

<u>Revelation 18:23-24</u>: And the light of a candle shall shine no more at all in thee; and the voice of the bridegroom and of the bride shall be heard no more at all in thee; for thy merchants were the great men of the earth for by thy sorceries were all nations deceived. And in her was found the blood of prophets, and of saints, and of all that were slain upon the earth. (KJV)

<u>I Peter 3:5</u>: For in the past, the Holy Women (Spiritual Royals) who put their hope (trust) in God (*Heaven Energy*) also beautified (action that creates health/vitality) themselves in this way, submitted to their own husbands (Ancient Custom(s)). (Interpretation inserted) (HCS)

<u>Mark 2:20</u>: But the time will come when the Groom is taken away from them, and then they will fast in that day. (KJV)

<u>Matthew 25:5, 10</u>: Since the Groom was delayed, they all became drowsy and fell asleep. <u>v. 10</u>: When they had gone to buy some (oil), the Groom arrived. Then those who were ready went in with him to the wedding banquet, and the door was shut. (KJV)

<u>II Samuel 17:3</u>: And bring all the people back to you. When everyone returns except the man you're seeking, all the people will be at peace. (HCS)

Bride/female is directing our attention to Spirit. Light of a candle is fire (Holy Spirit), the *Heaven Energy*. The People Group (*Spiritual Royals*) had possession of this Spirit Fire many years ago. The customs and skills that helped keep that Fire alive were sold or traded, as noted by the involvement of "merchants." The merchants who were great in influence, or became great through the sorcery (trickery) they added to the customs and skills they gained control over, deceived mankind. The sole proprietorship of the customs and skills was removed from the *Spiritual Royals* and placed in unskilled hands. The transfer resulted in the *Spiritual Royals* (original owners) being slain, extinct. The *Spiritual Royals* held the genetic code for Prophets and Saints and were put to death spiritually and in some cases literally.

When proper Spirit "food" is taken away, starvation of the Life once held inside the body dies. Without the customs that sustain health and vitality of life, the ability to live an Abundant Life is lost.

Mark and Matthew verses speak of timing. The bridegroom is what makes up the whole of Heaven Energy, Natural Healthcare and Wellness (the Jesus components) and the Christ transformation; this all adds up to Ancient Customs.

When the Ancient Customs return the *Spiritual Royals* will desire or long for what those customs offer, like a new bride longs to be with her new husband. Others will be unaware; out shopping around for ways to keep their body going (oil for lamps) elsewhere; they had to move on before the Ancient Customs were known or recognized. Oil burns by means of a fire but oil is not the fire itself. The actual Fire (Spirit) is due to return and those who have the *Star Dust* sparkle on the inside will know "it" is here; they are drawn to it and have an inner knowing about it. The day is approaching when the Ancient Holy Spirit Fire will be on Earth again. Miraculous things will take place. What has been here in the past four hundred years is not comparable to what is on the horizon. Once those who are identified as *Spiritual Royals* come together, the doors will shut. No outsiders will be allowed. The *Spiritual Royals* will be the only authentic carriers of the Ancient Holy Spirit Fire.

Threads: People Groups

CHRIST

Christ (author's definition): A term used to identify a particular form of internal change or transformation. The internal change progresses by a means of electrical conductivity that fuels various Life giving functions within the body, and is encompassed by different degrees of suffering. The Natural processes of the physical body, which result in a healing, or to sustain health.

I Peter 1:11: Searching what, or what manner of time the **Spirit** of Christ which was in them did signify, when it testified **beforehand** the sufferings of Christ, and the glory that should follow. (Emphasis added) (KJV)

I Peter 4:1-2: Forasmuch then as Christ hath suffered for us in the flesh, **arm yourselves likewise** with the same mind; for **he that hath suffered** in the flesh hath ceased from sin. (Emphasis added) (KJV)

Colossians 3:4: When Christ, who is our life, shall appear, then shall ye also appear with him in glory. (KJV)

Hebrews 9:26: So Christ was once offered to bear the sins of many; and unto them that look for him shall he appear the second time without sin unto salvation. (KJV)

Numbers 14:18: The Lord is longsuffering and of great mercy, forgiving iniquity and transgression, and by no means *clearing the guilty, visiting the iniquity of the fathers upon the children unto the third and fourth generation. (KJV)*

<u>Galatians 2:20</u>: *I am crucified with Christ; nevertheless I live; yet not I, but Christ liveth in me and the life which I now live in the flesh I live by the faith of the Son of God, who loved me, and gave himself for me. (KJV)*

<u>Hebrews 11:1</u>: *Now faith is the substance of things hoped for, the evidence of things not seen. (KJV)*

Christ is not a person. Jesus was identified with the Christ transformation.

It takes an element of some form of energy for anything to move, change or shift. Why the need for shift or change? To avoid disease and death of the physical body. No certificate or vocation can obtain Christ. There may be no visible change to an individual who has achieved a Christ transformation other than by countenance or a sense of knowing.

Jesus, Tribe of Judah, references a specific bloodline. We could say Judah has members in the *Star Dust* group. Judah is given the reputation of having strayed; he ended up off course, wandering in a strange territory. (We could call this strange territory medical intervention or food consumption alterations.) Jesus, generations later, comes on the scene to redirect the wandering Souls to their birthright path; the path of Christ transformation. Obviously, not everyone agreed with this approach.

Scrolling through the events Jesus encountered, crucified indicates challenging situations, a form of suffering resulting in death. Death can be a description for a natural physical death, death of habits, customs and lifestyles, or any number of other things. Natural Healthcare processes within the body is named "Jesus" in Scripture. A Natural healing process may require a level of toughing it out. Some situations may need the assistance of herbal remedies or nutritional supplements but does not include most remedies purchased at pharmacies. The removal of the Christ custom opened a door for new approaches that risk a result of permanent damage to the physical body, financial burden, and continual medical consultations or treatment. (i.e., surgeries that removed organs or glands). Humanity moved into a cycle of continuing physical ailment, decline, decay and disease. This cycle of medical intervention has developed the necessity for the physical body to undergo steps that would be challenging or in some cases impossible to overcome in order to achieve a Christ transformation and "live like Jesus."

An individual will go through some challenging, troubling and disturbing situations during a Christ transformation process. Falls in line with the "crucified with Christ" terminology. There is a piercing of what seems normal or beneficial to you or your body in order to bring necessary change. Life (vitality) is not all about what individuals often think it is about.

Christ transformation signifies the erasing of the Sin

imprints, self-inflicted and ancestor inherited, and is the only way to remove Sins.

Individuals not only have their own Sin baggage, they carry the Sin baggage of those up the bloodline. This creates many problems, physically, *E-motionally*, and even mentally, and all of this hinders the power of the Spirit within. The physical body ends up with various signals going off; one day they feel good, the next day they are down; they are healthy for months then suddenly they become deathly ill; they like Joey one day and the next day they don't. These signals come from 1-4 generations back through the ancestral road of travel and can be similar to notes on a keyboard played with no harmony; they do not mix well and end up sounding like music from a horror movie. These signals are within the cells in the blood and exist in every individual creating a situation of being dominated by some level of ancestor Sin. This is "bearing the Sins of many." There really is "power in the blood."

Through Jesus (Natural Healthcare) + Christ (suffering instead of intervening to allow the body to make necessary adjustments), an individual becomes Sin-free, cleaning out all the signals left in the blood that trickled down the generations, and the signals imprinted by their own thoughts or actions. In the arena of energy therapies this would be called a clearing. Erasing the old record. When the blood is clear of all of the excess chatter, an individual can think, feel, and live free, being who they were designed to be. They qualify for becoming a Bride. (II Corinthians 11:2)

The Return of Christ, the process that brings internal transformation, is soon to come. Humanity will progress to a state of living healthy, aging yet not decaying. Medical intervention is necessary for specific ailments or injuries; it should not be necessary for every day survival. People will eventually evolve into a position of not needing or requiring regular medical attention. After transformation, a maintenance regimen of Natural Healthcare would be required.

Challenges that unfold during a Christ transformation experience will change an individual's perspective, their reactions, their *E-motions*, their lifestyle and interactions with others, and more as the transformation progresses. Purging and refining by Fire are not necessarily welcomed. A person will most likely go through a Job type experience losing many things they are accustomed to having. If you can't take it, you won't make it through a Christ transformation.

Since mankind has not been living in a Christ transformation, where have they been living? Without Christ would be AntiChrist. Correct? When an individual does not have the classification of Christ transformation there's only one other title to be held. Guess we can toss aside Hollywood's version of the AntiChrist.

Jesus is Natural Healthcare; Christ is the transformation that allows the individual to advance to the use of solely Natural Healthcare and *Heaven Energy*.

Some current ruling spirits will need to be set aside when an individual decides to accept the way of Christ. According to Hebrews, Christ is a combination of Rest and Faith. Rest is a form of trusting; no worry, just relax into it. Faith is the futuristic dream type of hope in something that is not yet tangible. You need both Rest and Faith to get through a Christ transformation. You cannot join a group in an attempt to obtain Christ transformation. The transformation is earned by individual trial by Fire.

So what are these "things not seen" referenced in Hebrews 11? This statement is not referencing setting your mind on being a millionaire and hoping it will happen. Things not seen can be things that take place inside the body. It is the things that you feel or sense but cannot see, on most occasions anyway. Movement of *Heaven Energy* is not seen, the results of it may be seen but it alone is not visible. (*II Corinthians 4:18*)

Having seen both sides of the coin, life inside a religion and life interacting with *Heaven Energy*, the term Christian appears to be misplaced.

Threads: Blood; Glory; Sin; Son of Man

COMMUNION

<u>Communion</u>: The sharing of intimate thoughts and feelings, esp. when the exchange is on a mental or spiritual level.

<u>Prefix-"Comm"</u>: With or together.

<u>Union</u>: The action or fact of joining or being joined, esp. in a political context. A club, society or association formed by people with a common interest or purpose.

<u>I Corinthians 10:20</u>: *But I say, that the things which the Gentiles sacrifice, they sacrifice to devils, and not to God; and I would not that ye should have fellowship with devils. (Gentiles: foreign/foreigner) (HCS)*

<u>II Corinthians 6:14</u>: *Be ye not unequally yoked together with unbelievers; for what fellowship hath righteousness with unrighteousness? And what communion hath light with darkness? (KJV)*

<u>Luke 22:17-18</u>: *And He took the cup, and gave thanks, and said, Take this, and divide it among yourselves; for I say unto you, I will not drink of the fruit of the vine, until the kingdom of God shall come. (KJV)*

<u>1 Peter 2:9</u>: *But ye are a chosen generation, a royal*

priesthood, an holy nation, a peculiar people; that ye should shew forth the praises of him who hath called you out of darkness into his marvelous light. (KJV)

Communion is the act of sharing time, projects, job ideas, or efforts with people who have a common interest. There's been a whole lot of hanging out with the wrong crowd going on according to I and II Corinthians. The wrong crowd may be your current circle of influence.

Jesus adds an important caveat on communion activity in Luke 22. Drink is something that is taken in ("taken in" being by observing or by participation) that brings refreshment; a cup is the experience; and wine is the *Spiritual Royals* from the vine/bloodline that are aged in wisdom. Fine wines are aged well. Setting aside any temptation to be narrow minded, this verse is saying that Jesus (Natural Healthcare) has not had a group to hang out with for many years; the Spiritual level of communion left. Once the Jesus + Christ concepts are put into place and running well, like a well-oiled engine, He comes to hang out! This brings up the thought: Since Jesus hasn't been among us, who has?

The Kingdom of God gets ushered in by the *Spiritual Royals*, the "chosen generation." These *Spiritual Royals* with *Star Dust* in their blood begin the process of resurrecting the Ancient Customs and Ways, and those Ancient Customs and Ways evolve into "the Way."

The Ancient Customs and Ways, in part involve Natural ways of growing food and addressing healthcare needs. Once the Natural ways are given the respect and position they deserve, it will elevate the connection to Heaven Energy, which will result in Communion (a form of sharing) with Jesus (Natural Healthcare).

The People Group Jesus would commune with have been scattered; have lost the Ancient Customs and Ways and have not been in Communion amongst themselves, let alone have Jesus in their midst. The People Group who bring back and believe in Ancient Customs and Ways will bond together. They have a common thread and will share Communion. Jesus will finally have a group to hang out with!

As stated in Ecclesiastes: *To every thing there is a season, and a time to every purpose under the Heaven.* Sounds a bit like fate.

<u>Threads</u>: Ancient Ways; Blood; Sin

DEAD, DEATH, DIE, DIED and SLEEP, SLEPT

Lazarus: God has helped, gave support to. (God = Heaven Energy)

Death: A permanent irreversible cessation of all biological functions.

Die/Died: Activity ceased.

Sleep/Slept: A natural, periodic state of rest for the mind and body in which the eyes usually close and consciousness is completely or partially lost so that there is a decrease in bodily movement and responsiveness to external stimuli.

Metaphor of Sleep/Slept: Being unaware of what is going on around you. (i.e., "Boy, you slept through that one didn't you?")

Glory: Great honor, praise, renown.

John 11:4, 11, 13-14: When Jesus heard that, he said, This sickness is not unto death, but for the glory of God, that the Son of God might be glorified thereby. v. 11: These things said he: and after that he saith unto them, Our friend Lazarus sleepeth; but I go, that I may awake him out of sleep. v. 13-14: Howbeit Jesus spake of his death: but they thought that he had spoken of taking of rest in sleep. Then said Jesus unto them plainly, Lazarus is dead. (KJV)

How could a human be "dead," yet after a few days rise to life? Physically it is impossible; the natural body would begin to decay. Why do these verses seem to present confusion? There are a few details in the story of Lazarus that need a closer look.

Skeletal highlights of the story of Lazarus: There is something going on inside Lazarus that he is unaware of; what is evident to others is the resulting symptoms. This "something" is going on under the surface, internal, referenced by being in a tomb, not in plain sight. Jesus knew what was going on and knew that this "something" issue had been there awhile and had recently produced visible symptoms. Jesus knew the status of Lazarus and that another day or two in his condition would not cause Lazarus to depart to the sweet by-and-by. When the physical body shows symptoms, underlying issues have been brewing for a while. The blood becomes contaminated, cells begin to struggle, die off or absorb the toxin that is floating around in the blood stream. The toxic cells can reflect a form of death. There is no light or life left within the cell and therefore the result is darkness, death. Dark cells eventually lead to disease, which then leads to death, either of the cell, or of the physical body. When Jesus Christ (Natural Healthcare + the accompanying Christ transformation) comes on the scene, Lazarus is cured of this "something." Jesus shows up, the death component leaves resulting in Lazarus being raised to life. There is a shift that does not take place when a standard medical intervention is applied. Potential deadly situations leave when the Natural Healthcare and transformation named Jesus Christ, arrives. The process Lazarus goes through results in him graduating to a Son of God (verses a Son of Man). Son of God would indicate a form of *Heaven Energy* has taken up residence in Lazarus. We can safely assume the "something" in Lazarus was related to an overabundance of *E-motions*.

In the Old Testament there are several references to when King so-and-so passed-on he "slept" (with his fathers, meaning ancestors). In these verses slept references a physical death, yet there is a whisper of a different kind of death. There is some element of an unconscious life. Otherwise, the verses would just state that King so-and-so died and was buried. Seems we have a situation where King so-and-so has abandoned the body, but a state of unconscious life still exits.

Do these various references to some "sleep" and some "died" represent a possibility that there are varying conclusions when it comes to moving on from this conscious life on Earth? Contrary to popular belief, it is possible that some die, meaning no longer have any form of life after the physical body shuts down, and some have a continuing form that is unconsciously existing out "there" somewhere. This may answer how varying religions treat death differently holding to different conclusions on what happens after the Spirit essence (ghost) exits the physical body. Some believe there is nothing after death; once the physical body shuts down its "lights out" forever. And then there are many who believe everyone goes on to either a delightful eternity or a dark eternity. Bottom line, no one has the ability to expand on the possible experience until they've been "there."

<u>Threads</u>: Life; Son of Man; Soul

FIRST ADAM/LAST ADAM

<u>I Corinthians 15:45</u>: *And so it is written, The first man Adam was made a living soul; the last Adam was made a quickening spirit. (KJV)*

<u>II Corinthians 4:18</u>: *While we look not at the things which are seen, but at the things which are not seen; for the things which are seen are temporal; but the things which are not seen are eternal. (KJV)*

<u>1 Timothy 2:13-14</u>: *For Adam was first formed, then Eve. And Adam was not deceived, but the woman being deceived was in the transgression. (KJV)*

Simply put, the first Adam was flesh, visible, tangible. The second go-round is Spirit activity, Heaven Energy; not seen, yet felt or sensed. The Second Adam is symbolic of the previously described assignments of Jesus and Christ. Scripture describes this returning process as appearing in the cloud on a white horse. In a literal sense, this is quite unlikely. A strategy of picking apart the pieces and digging a little deeper provides a more realistic interpretation.

What does the White Horse represent? Jesus is Natural Healthcare; a horse is Power and White Horses were the choice of Royals. Clouds hold moisture particles and those particles hold frequencies giving the clue that it is an invisible, to the naked eye, energetic component to the picture.

Taking in a little different view, let's look at what that power that is coming through the clouds might look like. While the actual events of Adam and Eve being in a Garden and encountering a talking snake are still up for debate, today the passage of text needs focus on the Spiritual message. This verse does <u>not</u> say "Eve being deceived;" it states "the woman," referencing a spiritual issue. The deception came toward the Spirit, the intuition was removed, logical thought processing applied and the walk through the Valley of the Shadow of Death began. Deception led to many years of disease and death, the Valley experience. When a transgression against the Spirit is made, it separates the individual from the source that feeds the personal Spirit. You become unplugged from your energy source. This story represents the following:

There was a time in Ancient history when people lived healthy. They had natural energy (not caffeine driven) and properly functioning immune systems that can all be compared to living in the Garden of Eden. Hundreds of years ago a spiritual influence of deception, amongst other things, came into the picture that resulted in the dismantling of the Abundant Life they had. You could say the snake came on the scene. The ability to sense, know and trust an inner knowing, gut feeling or intuition is part of what will return through *Spiritual Royals*, along with an ability to live by means of Natural Healthcare versus medical intervention. No more pain, suffering, sorrow or tears. Adam reflects the physical aspect of life while Eve represents the Spiritual Life.

To graduate to the Second Adam, the physical body must progress through the transitions (Christ and Jesus) and become the recipient of the "incorruptible seed" (healthy energized cells that classify as becoming a Son of God). This brings forth the spiritual Adam housed inside the physical Adam (body). At this point, the cycle has been made back to the Garden of Eden. This process cannot take place when logical thinking is at play.

Threads: Heaven; Wheels

Suggested Research: Uffington White Horse, Oxfordshire, England

GLORY

<u>Glory</u>: A highly praiseworthy asset. Great honor, praise or distinction; renown.

<u>Celestial</u>: Of or relating to the sky or physical universe as understood in astronomy.

<u>Terrestrial</u>: Living or growing on land or in the ground; not aquatic, arboreal, or epiphytic; of or relating to the earth inhabitants.

<u>II Peter 1:17</u>: *For he received from God the Father honor and glory, when there came such a voice to him from the excellent glory, "this is my beloved Son, in whom I am well pleased." (KJV)*

<u>I Peter 4:14</u>: *If ye be reproached for the name of Christ, happy are ye; for the Spirit of Glory and of God resteth upon you; on their part he is evil spoken of but on your part he is glorified. (KJV)*

<u>I Corinthians 15:40-41</u>: *There are celestial bodies and bodies terrestrial; but the glory of the celestial is one, and the glory of the terrestrial is another. There is one glory of the sun, and another glory of the moon, and another glory of the stars; for one star differeth from another star in glory. (KJV).*

II Corinthians 3:18: We all with unveiled faces, are looking as in a mirror, at the glory of the Lord and are being transformed into the same image from glory to glory; this is from the Lord who is the Spirit. (KJV)

The word Glory is used to describe the resulting manifestation of Spiritual growth or change at the conclusion of a Christ suffering and transformation; to host a greater measure of Heaven Energy, versus human effort, within the physical body. Glory is achieved through the process of Christ transformation. An experience where you get to decide whom the better one to listen to is, the pressures of society, or God.

Looking at I Corinthians 15 raises the question of whether at the time a Glorified Spirit exits the physical body, does it become a part of or co-exist with or amongst the celestial or terrestrial; the sun, moon or stars? Considering Heaven is the sky (Universe), and Hell is the atmosphere that rules the Earth, then is it possible after physical death a living Glorified Spirit would be present amongst the Universe? Sure beats some of the other options that have been taught. What about the thought of those who have the Star Dust in their blood? Do they go to Heaven (the cosmos) and exist there? The ones described in other Topics who have the natural abilities to work with Spirit activity vs. Earth activity, do they become a star? All interesting thoughts if nothing else.

Threads: Son of Man

HEAVEN

Heaven: The sky or universe as seen from the earth; the firmament. The abode of God, the angels and the souls of those who are granted salvation. An eternal state of communion with God; everlasting bliss.

I John 2:15: *Love not the world, neither the things that are in the world. If any man love the world, the love of the Father is not in him. (KJV)*

John 3:19: *And this is the condemnation, that light is come into the world and men loved darkness rather than light because their deeds were evil. (KJV)*

Isaiah 14:12: *How are thou fallen from heaven, O Lucifer, son of the morning! How art thou cut down to the ground, which didst weaken the nations! (KJV)*

A Scientist would have a little different twist for a definition of Heaven that might include references to atoms, particles, plasma, waves and all that fancy stuff many individuals outside of a Science degree don't think about. Common references to Heaven (where God is) in religion and Science are Power and Energy, respectively, different terminology but the same idea. Religion says Power (or God); Science says Energy, that "stuff" that is attached to tiny droplets of moisture that floats around in the cosmos. Bottom line is, obviously I am no Scientist, but there is activity in the Heavens that house a charge that is called Energy or Power. That charge is also called frequency or vibration. Sound, thoughts, words and actions, all record in those tiny droplets. (See, *Dr. Masaru Emoto's Water Experiment*). There is activity "out there" that can produce sound. Mix the proper portions of the elements that are available and you have an atmosphere of Heaven. That Heaven can interact with life on Earth. "On Earth as it is in Heaven." Sound familiar?

Personal connection with Heaven Energy can just happen for some individuals. This is where the term bliss comes in. *II Corinthians 5:5: And the One who prepared us for this very purpose is God, who gave us the Spirit as a down payment.* Like an old radio with a dial needle, the needle has to be set just right in order to have a clear connection. Star Dust is what I call this code in the blood that comes from God and allows connection to the Heaven Energy.

If "up there" is Heaven, what is "down here," besides Earth? Could Earth, not the planet itself but the atmosphere that has come about upon it, be what Scripture refers to as Hell? What if Hell is a supercharged atmosphere of evil created by human activity on Earth? Idea seems to go along with the verses that speak of loving the world.

It is well received that there is no evil in Heaven and evil resides in Hell; that's where the darkness and scary things are, right? According to John 3, that darkness and evil is where mankind is and man resides on Earth. Would a shift in personal priorities change the atmosphere on Earth and allow Heaven to rain blessings on us? For sure, somewhere at some point in time, activities took place that caused a weakness that permeates around the world.

So if Heaven is the home of components that make Energy and Power, and Hell is the atmosphere influencing life being lived out on Earth, what happens to an individual's Spirit when they die?

Threads: Dead; Glory

I AM

<u>I AM</u>: Presence of the Spirit; the Spirit has arrived.

<u>Moses</u>: The root meaning of the name Moses is quite extensive on Arabim-publications.com. I list only a few descriptions they present: A lifted up one; bear or carry; to take away or deceive. A ruler or chief; mist or vapor. Clouds + a loan; to lend. Guile. Hidden or covered.

<u>Moses</u> (author's definition): an exalted, ruling invisible (unseen) spirit; the description of how things fall into their place; The Laws of Nature.

<u>Exodus 3:14</u>: *God replied to Moses **I AM WHO I AM**; this is what you are to say to the Israelites: I AM has sent me to you. (KJV)*

<u>I Corinthians 15:10</u>: *But by the grace of God, **I am what I am**; and his grace which was bestowed upon me was not in vain; but I laboured more abundantly than they all; yet not I but the grace of God which was with me. (KJV)*

<u>II Corinthians 11:22</u>: *Are they Hebrews? So Am I. Are they Israelites? So Am I. Are they seed of Abraham? So Am I. (KJV)*

I AM speaks of the descendants of Jacob (Israelites) who have been entrusted with a fragment of the ultimate power that created all things; the people with *Star Dust* in their blood. The picture that comes to mind is that of a falling star that takes up residence in a fetus. Not every physical body has this. Some humans are the result of cells that split and grow into a baby that has a Soul; they may contain a level of Spirit but not a *Star Dust* level. When a person has reached "I AM" it means they have completed the Christ transformation, have adopted the Jesus Natural Healthcare and Wellness and have a personal relationship or interaction with God. There body now functions on the acts of the Laws of Nature. Israelites possess a fragment of the Spirit that not every human does.

I AM appears to indicate Israelites have a gift of functioning by and with the Laws of Nature. How? Once the physical body completes the Christ transformation and adopts Jesus Natural Healthcare, the physical body gains the ability to shed harmful cells, process food properly, encounter toxins or infections and rid itself of them. A good visual is a healthy tree. The tree receives from Nature (Sun; rain; nutrients from soil) that supplies it with the ability to fight off invaders and grow. A tree, depending on the species, can live hundreds of years. When the physical body is supplied with solely beneficial nutrients that it needs to keep the natural processes going, it will live a life here on Earth longer as well. (120 years. (Deuteronomy 34:7))

Threads: Israel; People Groups

ISRAEL/ISRAELITE

Israel: (Arabim-Publications.com descriptions) God; rigidity resulting from the absorption and retention of liquids. Chief ruler; princess or noble lady, a ruling class collectively. Stubborn; umbilical cord (connection); mystery describes Jacob's actions with the angel (Genesis 32:29 and Hosea 12:4); retention of knowledge. To fill and release; juice of grapes; a weapon or body armor. Link between the physical and political and intellectual. For additional in depth description see Arabim-Publications.com, Israel.

Isaiah 41:8: But thou, Israel, art my servant, Jacob whom I have chosen, the seed of Abraham my friend. (KJV)

Isaiah 48:12: Harken unto me, O Jacob and Israel, my called; I am he; I am the first, I also am the last. (KJV)

Zechariah 12:7: The Lord also shall save the tents of Judah first, that the glory of the house of David and the glory of the inhabitants of Jerusalem do not magnify themselves against Judah. (KJV)

I Samuel 16:12: And he sent, and brought him in. Now he was ruddy and withal of a beautiful countenance, and *goodly to look to. And the Lord said, Arise, anoint him; for this is he. (KJV)*

In a nutshell, the root meaning of Israel lays out what is described in many Topics in this book. The selected class that chiefly rule. Chiefly rule what?

A class of people that chiefly rule ("ruling class") that Judah will be first to take position in. This ruling class has the ability to access the *Heaven Energy* and deliver appropriate contents to Earth. Jacob ascending and descending by way of the ladder reflects the access to Heaven and back to Earth. This access is referenced in the Arabim-publication definition as umbilical cord. The Spiritual umbilical cord provides not only a point of access but also a form of nourishment and protection. It is a link between the physical Earth realm and the invisible Spirit realm. Jacob's wrestling match with the angel reflects struggling with the way life will be walked out from then on (Genesis 32).

The ruling class of people have a choice as to whether they will follow the guidelines prescribed in order to have the access to the *Heaven Energy* or not, whether they personally carry it or they just access it through one who does. The choice may seem simple, yet guidelines for remaining a member of a ruling class beyond the genetic code often goes against the grain of society. There is a whisper of the exact situation I am attempting to describe in the recent events of Prince Harry and his lovely family no longer living under the roof of the Royal Castle. Life in the world can be challenging when you are a Royal, whether physically or spiritually. Much of the busyness of society does not host an environment healthy for a Spiritual ruling class. Some difficult choices may need to be made. Then again, sticking with what is considered a normal lifestyle when you are genetically a Spiritual ruling class member will eventually have consequences. The Spiritual ruling class is not cut out of a common cloth.

References to Israel or Israelite in Scripture are referencing a specific People Group that became scattered. Some Israelites may reside in the actual Country of Israel, but many do not. Israelite is not referencing a religion. I have yet to find a reference to Jacob (aka Israel) taking up any religion. There are etiquettes to be followed but not religion.

Any reference to an obvious physical difference between the Spiritual ruling class and others can be found in Genesis 12:11; II Samuel 14:27; Esther 1:11 and 2:7; I Kings 1:3 where Sarai/Sarah, Tamar and Esther, by name, are all referred to as a "fair woman." Song of Solomon speaks of the "fair damsel;" Kings sought after a "fair damsel," one of pale or ivory complexion. Birth mothers of Israelites had fair complexion.

David was a smaller framed person than his brothers; he is also described as "ruddy", meaning having reddish tones. The reddish tones are likely referring to hair color, that of a chestnut, or brownish red color. Having red cheeks can also be a description of ruddy. Fair complexions express red cheeks. The story of David and Goliath reflects the power placed within the selected fair complexion, red cheeked, chestnut hair individuals that can take down great obstacles, called giants.

Who is this Spiritual ruling class? Descendants of Judah first, with other Israelites to follow. Judah is mentioned separate from the Israelites many places in Scripture. How are the descendants of Judah recognized today? It is unlikely many family trees stretch back to the days of Jesus. What can be done is connect the dots.

- Small body frame; petite; (King David)
- Fair complexion; (Esther; Sarah; Tamar)
- Hair of Chestnut or Brown/Red tones; (David)
- Blue Eyes (Eyes a flaming fire. Eyes are not yellow or orange so the flame color referenced is blue.)
- Lion of the Tribe of Judah; (Britain)
- Uffington White Horse, Oxfordshire, England (indicative of region of Ancient Customs)
- The English have a history of being proficient horsemen.

Threads: People Groups; White Horse

JESUS

Jesus: To save or deliver.

Propitiate: To gain or regain the favor of; to disarm.

I John 2:2: And he is the propitiation for our sins; and not for ours only, but also for the sins of the whole world. (KJV)

From the time of His birth, Jesus has been a symbol of Natural Healthcare. Frankincense and Myrrh were highly sought after for medicinal use in Ancient times. (*Matthew 2:11*)

Mark 5:31 describes the experience Jesus had when the woman with the issue of blood touched His robe and the "power" left Him. This reference to blood connects with the frequencies of Sin that develop into disease. If you recall, the woman had been to many physicians only to receive a loss of money and no remedy. The power that was present in Jesus is what healed her. That power is what can heal people today, there's just been a lack of knowing how to obtain it.

The Natural Healthcare is what will deliver an individual

from the cycles of decline; the Natural Healthcare that joins with the Christ transformation.

Several stories in Scripture reflect Jesus applying various Natural means to assist a process of healing. From the use of saliva and mud to instructions to go down into the depths of the dirty river waters of *E-motions*, Natural approaches to health and recovery were the way Jesus worked.

John's reference to "the whole world" fits with the fact that every human has imprints from ancestors that could have been from all over the world.

Threads: Ancient Ways; Bread of Life; Christ

LIFE

Life: A state of an organism characterized esp. by capacity for metabolism, growth, reaction to stimuli, and reproduction.

Life (author's definition): A continuous flow or cycle initiated by the breath and electrical conductivity within the physical body that maintains vitality. The process the body naturally goes through to process food, expel unusable substances, and provide growth. Anything outside of this would be classified as a measure of death.

Luke 17:33: Whosoever shall seek to save his life shall lose it; and whosoever shall lose his life shall preserve it. (KJV)

Luke 12:23: For life is more than food and the body more than clothing. (KJV)

Relying on what is contained within the medicine cabinet or pharmacy will eventually cause the vitality (Life) to be lost. Man-made remedies often interfere with the Natural processes of the body. There are times the body needs to process invaders on its own, or with minimal interference. It takes effort, time and money to properly feed the body and to keep it active at an appropriate level. If one chooses to have a garden as a food supply, this takes time. Today, much of the food served in restaurants is overdosed with sodium and not health-worthy for those who are assigned to Spiritual work. Preparing meals from your home may become necessary and will likely result in missing out on some social events. This describes a fraction of what a current day "losing ones life in order to save it" might look like. Today people desire what is quick or easy. The steps required to achieve and support a healthy, Sin free body takes sacrificing some of the "norms."

Threads: Blood; Dead

MYSTERIES

<u>Mysteries</u>: Occupation, trade, office, profession, calling, art, craft. Plural in ancient religions; rites known and practiced by certain initiated persons only; consisting of purifications, sacrificial offerings, processions, songs, dances, dramatic performances, and the like.

<u>Mysteries</u> (author's definition): The series of events that have been lost or hidden and become difficult to recover. Messages written in a code that requires specific skills or tools to understand.

<u>Ephesians 1:9</u>: Having made known unto us the mystery of his will, according to his good pleasure which he hath purposed in himself. (KJV)

<u>Ephesians 3:3</u>: How that by revelation he made known unto me the mystery; ...(KJV)

<u>Colossians 1:26-27</u>: Even the mystery which hath been hid from ages and from generations, but now is made manifest to his saints; To whom God would make known what is the riches of the glory of this mystery among the Gentiles; which is Christ in you, the hope of glory. (KJV)

<u>James 1:17</u>: Every good gift and every perfect gift is from

above, and cometh down from the Father of lights, with whom is no variableness, neither shadow of turning. (KJV)

Leviticus 17:14: For it is the life of all flesh; the blood of it is for the life thereof; therefore I said unto the children of Israel, Ye shall eat the blood of no manner of flesh; for the life of all flesh is the blood thereof; whosoever eateth it shall be cut off. (KJV)

I Corinthians 15:38-39: But God giveth it a body and as it hath pleased him, and to every seed his own body. (KJV)

I Corinthians 7:7: For I would that all men were even as I myself. But every man hath his proper gift of God, one after this manner, and another after that. (KJV)

Romans 12:6-8: Having then gifts differing according to the grace that is given to us, whether prophecy, let us prophesy according to the proportion of faith; or ministry, let us wait on our ministering; or he that teacheth, on teaching; or he that exhorteth on exhortation; he that giveth, let him do it with simplicity; he that ruleth, with diligence; he that sheweth mercy, with cheerfulness. (KJV)

I Peter 4:10: As every man hath received the gift, even so minister the same one to another, as good stewards of the manifold grace of God. If any man speak, let him speak as the oracles of God; if any man minister, let him do it as of the ability which God giveth; that God in all things may be glorified through Jesus Christ, to whom be praise and dominion for ever and ever. Amen. (KJV)

There are several verses in Scripture that reference Mystery or Mysteries. Appears, even from the few verses above, that there has been specific information pertaining to assignments or official positions that was written in a code of mysteries. Now, what was lost will begin to surface.

Example of what was lost:

Adam and Eve had a perfect life; life in the Garden of vitality of Life where cycles of physical and Spiritual benefit and pleasure would take place. Maintaining the Garden involved time and effort. When well kept, life would move along as it was designed.

Influences and pressures arise and trigger Adam and Eve to step outside their God assignment of tending to the cycles of life within the Garden. Grass appeared much greener on the other side where protocols, social events and schedules did not appear as stressful. They follow their thoughts and emotions to a more common way of living, ceasing their Garden assignment. By evening, God is aware that Adam and Eve were slacking on their assignments so He takes a stroll through the Garden to address them on the subject. After brief questioning, God explains that their choice for change will cost them their life(style) and has them ushered out of their once thriving and bountiful life. Separation takes place, resulting in struggle, physical setbacks, sickness and hardships for Adam and Eve.

Generations come and go and the longer Adam and Eve remain outside of their Garden life, choosing what they thought would be easier and more beneficial, the generational line becomes further and further away from the Garden life, resulting in physically and Spiritually weak descendants. What happened?

God assigned a protocol for a way the physical body was to be nourished and cared for that would produce a productive, healthy life. This Life is reflected in the symbol of the Garden.

As time proceeds and Abraham, Isaac and Jacob enter the scene, specification for nourishment and lifestyle narrow down to a specific bloodline. Scripture begins to give instruction to specific People Groups when it comes to food intake and so on. Once the 12 Sons of Jacob enter the scene, it gets even more specific. Lifestyle, hygiene, food intake instructions split amongst the 12 tribes, dependent upon the blessing received from Jacob. Here is where the meaning of names is important. The meaning of the name combined with the story line for a particular Son of Jacob will unfold the various guidelines and responsibilities for people today. In the Holy Bible, the descendants of Jacob (aka Israel) are the main focus. Other forms of Ancient text may provide instructions for people outside of the bloodlines of Abraham, Isaac and Jacob.

Maintaining a pure bloodline could be one reason why it was common to marry within the Tribe (family). It kept the future generations clean and powerful for God assignments. When a person steps outside of what is naturally in the blood (codes implanted by God) life, work, relationships and health become a struggle. These God assignments are not what are granted by a church or education. These assignments are in the BLOOD. God has the original copyright for Spiritual work.

Attempting to escape the blood imprinted God assignment may be tolerable for a given time but will not resonate with the song being sung in the blood. Escape is what the *Spiritual Royals* People Group tried hundreds of years ago and catastrophe within the scope of the Spiritual interaction between Heaven and Earth was the result. When the wrong people attempt to handle assignments that don't belong to them, the whole world can suffer. Things simply do not sync up.

Leviticus 17 holds a mystery with respect to what should be eaten and what should be avoided. This instruction is Spirit assignment specific and you must know who you are to know whether eating meat is good for you or not. Improper food consumption is one of the components that lead to a separation from "God". Eventually the *Star Dust* power within the cells runs out when it is not provided the proper food. Being cut off from the Spiritual assignment in the blood can result in evil taking its place. There are dietary restrictions for certain bloodlines. (See also, I Samuel 16:14)

Investigating an ancestral bloodline can be interesting. Becoming aware of where ancestors lived and researching the history of that culture can be quite profound. Those with the blood imprints for being a Medium or Mediator between Heaven and Earth have their roots in a particular region. Having ancestral information can bring some "aha" and some "oh no" revelations. Whispers of your ancestors may be evident within your own life experience.

Will siblings of the same parents have the same assignment or skill? No. There can be siblings from the same parents and one child can have *Earth Dust* and one can have *Star Dust*. Meaning, one is encoded with what it takes to have a career or make money, the hunter, gatherer category; then another child can be born with the *Star Dust* in their blood meaning they will be workers with the Spirit and jobs that do not involve working with Spirit/Energy drain them physically; activities outside of their energy environment can be tiring for them.

One bloodline versus another bloodline does not mean one Tribe or People Group is less important or more important; the same is true with *Earth Dust* people versus *Star Dust* people. Scripture gives specific instructions to those with *Star Dust* Spiritual assignments they are to do. Not every bloodline has the Spiritual work assignment.

Threads: Israel; People Groups

PASSOVER

<u>Jew</u>: To praise; to be praise-worthy; splendor, majesty, vigor, glory or honor.

<u>John 11:55</u>: And the Jews' Passover was nigh at hand: and many went out of the country, up to Jerusalem for the Passover to purify themselves. (KJV)

<u>II Chronicles 35:18</u>: And there was no passover like to that kept in Israel from the days of Samuel the prophet; neither did all the kings of Israel keep such a passover as Josiah kept, and the priests, and the Levites, and all Judah and Israel that were present, and the inhabitants of Jerusalem. (KJV)

Passover is the purification through Christ transformation required in order for the Death Angel to drive on past when it reaches your residence, residence being your physical body. Passover is a mirrored image of the bitterness and hardships experienced in order to cleanse the harmful Sin imprints from the blood that results in a life free from the patterns of decay and decline.

All Sin imprints from ancestors or personal experiences must be erased from the blood before escape from death is achieved. The physical body will cease to function in the natural at some point in time. The Spirit ("Ghost") inside the physical body is what will live on. Without the Jesus and Christ processes described, the light of the Spirit can go out. "This little light of mine, I'm going to let it shine" is a part of reaching the point of being passed by and not swallowed up by the decline of the Spirit within.

Jews points to a specific group of individuals, who can achieve a Sin free status and advance into glory, not a religion.

Praise connects to the breath, "Let everything that has breath praise the Lord." Breathing a specific way brings movement to the internal processes of the body; a mirror image is the wind. The breath assists in Sin imprints being removed. Glory is achieved and maintained through the Christ transformation process coupled with Natural Healthcare (Jesus). "Christ in me, the hope of glory."

Threads: Christ; Glory; Israel; People Groups

PEOPLE GROUPS
(TRIBE)

Adopt: To take up and practice or use as one's own; to accept formally and put into effect.

Isaiah 5:13: Therefore, **my people** are gone into captivity, because they have no knowledge: and their honourable men are famished, and their multitude dried up with thirst. (Emphasis added) (KJV)

Zechariah 12:7: The Lord also shall save the tents of **Judah first**, that the glory of the house of David and the Glory of the inhabitants of Jerusalem do not magnify themselves against Judah. (*Emphasis added*) (KJV)

Nehemiah 7:5: And my God put into mine heart to gather together the nobles, and the rulers, and the people, that they might be **reckoned by genealogy**. And I found a register of the genealogy of them, which came up at the first, and found written therein. (Emphasis added) (KJV)

Leviticus 4:27: And if any one of the **common people** sin through ignorance, while he doeth somewhat against any of the commandments of the Lord concerning things which ought not to be done, and be guilty;... (Emphasis added) (KJV)

I Kings 13:33: After this thing, Jeroboam returned not from his evil way but made again of the lowest of the people, priests of the high places: whosoever would, he consecrated him, and he became one of the priests of the high places. (See also, I Kings 12:31) (KJV)

Esther 2:16: So Esther was taken unto King Ahasuerus into his house royal in the tenth month, which is the month Tebeth, in the seventh year of his reign. (KJV)

Ephesians 1:5: Having predestined us unto the adoption of children by Jesus Christ to himself, according to the good pleasure of his will. (KJV)

Romans 9:4: Who are Israelites; to whom pertaineth the adoption and the glory and the covenants, and the giving of the law, and the service of God and the promises. (KJV)

Romans 8:23: And not only they, but ourselves also, which have the firstfruits of the Spirit, even we ourselves groan within ourselves, waiting for the adoption, to wit, the redemption of our body. (KJV)

I Peter 2:9: But ye are a chosen generation, a royal priesthood, an holy nation, a peculiar people; that he should shew forth the praises of him who hath called you out of darkness into his marvelous light. (KJV)

Isaiah 5:13: Therefore, my people will go into exile for lack of understanding; those of high rank will die of hunger and the common people will be parched with thirst. (*Emphasis added*) (KJV)

II Corinthians 11:22: Are they Hebrews? So am I. Are they Israelites? So am I. Are they the seed of Abraham? So am I. (KJV)

A game-changer to the entire text of the Holy Bible is

held in identification of different People Groups. To date I have identified three distinct People Groups. With that, not every instruction or command applies to each People Group or individual. Individuals must identify the People Group (Tribe) they belong to before they have the ability to know which instructions are directed to them.

The ability to truly "know who you are" has been lost. Tribes lived together; they married within their Tribe. Today, many individuals, or their ancestors, have crossed country boundaries, taking up habitation with foreigners. They would be a "Gentile," living a lifestyle outside of what they were born into. Assignments and Scripture instructions can be Tribe specific, by the blood. Not blood type as we know today, but a code or imprint in blood that has not yet been discovered. That code distinguishes not only which Tribe a person is from, like a 23 and Me type genealogy result, but distinguishes a frequency (power) that Scripture describes as "God" appointed; a frequency that distinguishes who would be, to use Biblical terms, a priest, a servant or slave, or who was of the masses, or common folk. There is a form of identification that only God has known. It is hidden from the eyes and knowledge of mankind, yet mankind took on the role of assigning positions to various people resulting in situations similar to what is described in the verse above. (I Kings 13:33) Chaos can erupt when people are not put in their appropriate position. This is like placing a janitor or receptionist in a position of CEO or President and vice versa. Qualifications, which according to Scripture are held in the codes within the blood, determine who should have which position when it comes to Spiritual (*Heaven Energy*) assignments.

This does not mean one People Group or Tribe is better than or less than another. It simply reflects specific assignments that are prevalent within each particular group. There is no prejudice here. Be the star of the show within the group assignment that runs in your blood. You will get much farther than you would if you stress yourself trying to be something you were not intended (or encoded) to be.

The reference to "by Jesus Christ" means there is effort that will have to be applied in order to move from a servant to a position of priest or royal. It doesn't just happen. Like going through college, you have to apply time and effort to move up the ranks and graduate.

Worldly earmarks have been placed on what is considered good or bad, or highly praised, when it comes to careers, clothing style, type of residence or location where one lives. We can thank mankind for that. God sets people apart through a means of genetic codes to create a balance to the way the world goes around, so to speak. It takes all kinds. Striving for scholastic or career achievements and so on, has applied a pressure and social acceptability stamp onto certain obtainable titles. Those stamps are not of God's handiwork. This does not mean He wouldn't bless them, dependant upon whether you are of *Earth*

Dust or *Star Dust* and if you have chosen the path right for your genetic code. Those achieved titles may make an individual feel important or valuable for an increment of time but they do not grant an access to the *Heaven Energy*.

Three groups identified:

1) Royals
2) Masses/Common people
3) Servant/Slave

Threads: Israel; Mysteries

PRIEST

Priest: A person with authority to lead or perform ceremonies in some religions. A mediatory agent between humans and one or more deities.

Priest (author's definition): People assigned to render some form of sacrifice that benefits another.

Levite: A joining of two ends in a circular coiled or twisted band of leaves or twigs (laurel leaf); lending.

Nehemiah 3:45: Take the Levites instead of all the firstborn among the children of Israel, and the cattle of the Levites instead of their cattle; and the Levites shall be mine; I am the Lord. (KJV)

Any Priest title, or the like, that is recognized today has a root in human manufacturing. Here would be a good place to erase the imprinted thoughts of who or what a Priest is. The Priest referenced in Scripture is an appointed position that comes from God, meaning it is in the blood. This appointed position is not chosen by anyone, it is not earned through an educational training program, and cannot be purchased or sold. Scripture references a specific bloodline of people, who carry out specific duties connected to the realms of the invisible not only for themselves but for others as well.

Priests, known as Levites, share the load of experiences of those who are close to them; the physical and spiritual bodies of a Priest can become affected by another's reaction to an influence they encountered. <u>Example</u>:

Bob is experiencing a great deal of grief after the loss of his job. Bob has a close relationship to a person who has a genetic code of Priest (unidentified). Bob seems to feel better after he speaks with his Priest friend so Bob pays Priest a visit. At the conclusion of the visit, Bob leaves feeling the weight on his shoulders lift while the Priest begins to experience the load of the burden him/herself. This is where the Priest has the ability to take the *E-motions* of grief and submit them to the Heavens for clearing them away. The Priest absorbing the feelings of grief from the friend is a way for the Priest to identify what all needs to be cleared away. Sometimes people who are afflicted do not fully express what they feel simply because they are not aware of everything going on under the surface (internally). This is a great example of how Priests submitted sacrifices for Sin. Sin is a lingering or stuck negative *E-motion*. Priests act as a filter, helping purify the energy afflicting the other person. The duties involved in a Priest position are done in private; no audience, no recognition other than by someone noticing a change in how someone displays what they are feeling; Priests are an avenue in which change takes place. It is challenging work for a Priest. If they are not careful, it seems everywhere they go, they come home feeling weak or sickly simply because they picked up on someone's affliction unknowingly. This type of activity happens today and most are clueless what is happening.

Levite is a reference to those who have a built-in appointed position encoded in the livelihood of the blood for services of a Medium or Mediator between Heaven activity and Earth activity. What is not traceable and lacks visible proof are situations in which a seemingly ordinary person suffers and dies, not knowing they had a Priest genetic code in their blood. Their suffering could have helped erase health components of a threatening situation for another. The mystery of such a situation lies in the hands of God. The goal is to implement the ability for becoming a Priest. That skill was lost long ago.

Thread: Christ

SABBATH

<u>Sabbath</u>: Seventh day of the week (Friday, Saturday, or Sunday). A day of rest for the heart.

These are the common descriptions applied by human thoughts or history of the application that was attached to a word. The typical work six days, relax or rest on your Sabbath.

<u>Prefix Sab</u> (<u>saeb</u>): An informal Brit (British) person engaged in direct action to prevent a targeted activity.

The prefix Sab places a British person with an act of intercepting some form of an activity. British roots can carry a *Spiritual Royal* frequency.

<u>Bath</u>: Washing or soaking of all or part of the body. To immerse. City in England southwest of Bristol.

<u>Hagios</u> (<u>Greek</u>): Different from the world; likeness of nature with the Lord; to be different or special.

<u>Godesh</u> (<u>Hebrew</u>): Pure; morally blameless; set apart.

<u>Genesis</u>: The coming into being of something; to begin;

to become something; create, perform or occur; offspring or family.

<u>Acts 15:21</u>: *For since ancient times, Moses has had those who proclaim him in every city, and every Sabbath day he is read aloud in the synagogues. (KJV) (A description for Moses is found in the I AM Topic)*

<u>Ezekiel 46:1</u>: *Thus saith the Lord God; The gate of the inner court that looketh toward the east shall be shut the six working days; but on the Sabbath it shall be opened and in the day of the new moon it shall be opened. (KJV)*

The basic concept of Sabbath comes from the six days of creation through God's magnificent handiwork, followed by a day of rest. Let's look at Sabbath from a different direction.

Creation is a work of the *Heaven Energy* sourced by God. Energies were moving and shifting, bumping into each other at set increments of timing and this process was described as the six days of creation in Genesis. On day seven, God sat back and looked with admiration at the magnificence that became manifest due to the initiation, interaction and timing of *Heaven Energy*. God was the director of the play that unfolded. Day seven was used to take note of the works that had unfolded; time to tidy up some loose ends from the week's events and clear away any potential influences to His work; a gesture to clean the spiritual air of any likely negative invaders.

Stop, look, be amazed at how the ocean does not exceed

the established borders; how a baby develops from microscopic cells; how the flowers bloom and the birds scatter the seed that grows into forests; the Natural wonders that humans take for granted. What if taking time to be aware of the Natural wonders is God's message for keeping a Sabbath holy; a time to clear the air of any negative spiritual influence that came about through the events of the week; a time to take a break from the logical thinking attached to the week and tune into your inner knowing, the skill of using the intuition. The skill of how to follow that "hunch" or the "know that you know without any logical explanation" has been lost. Society is the Pharasee always wanting proof or logical reason. Take a day to get away from needing to know why or having a logical answer. Take time to "walk by faith and not by sight." (II Corinthians 5:7) Ezekiel 46:1 is talking about the interior functions of the body; gates reference the opening and closing of cells and how it coincides with a Sabbath and New Moon days.

Words are vibrations (Life and death are in the power of the tongue) and can create an atmosphere so taking time to clean up any invisible unwanted residue from the week's events is a Sabbath. Be aware of the invisible forces at work that provide a beautiful landscape, the air we breathe, a garden growing, and so much more. A Sabbath marks an awareness of shift and change that takes place by means of the invisible, the *Heaven Energy*. Be Still and Know that I Am God (Psalm 46:10).

A similar invisible *Heaven Energy* concept can be applied to the internal works of the physical body. The inside of the physical body requires a form of cleansing just as the outside of the physical body does. The interior cleansing takes place when the physical body is in a state of rest or relaxation. This allows the natural processes of the immune system, cells or circulation to do what they need to do in order to target a foreign cell or infection. This rest initiates the body to clean house and recharge.

The interior mechanisms of the physical body need time to reset, like a computer that requires a periodic reboot. For the interior mechanisms to reset and refresh, physical activity should be minimal, yet enough to assist circulation. The Sabbath is to take place one day out of every seven. Pick your day, any day of the week or weekend and make it your Sabbath. The Sabbath commitment can be challenging for many due to schedules, commitments, appointments and general activities. Rearrange the schedule in order to allow one full day free from electronics, family, extensive chores and other interruptions.

Threads: Breathe; I AM

SAINTS

<u>Saint</u>: Person officially recognized as being entitled to public veneration and capable of interceding for people on earth.

<u>Saint</u> (<u>author's definition</u>): Saint is an individual who becomes recognized by others, not appointed by others, as having a capability to be a Medium or Mediator of messages from deities as a service to others.

<u>Jude 3</u>: Beloved, when I gave all diligence to write unto you of the common salvation, it was needful for me to write unto you, and exhort you that ye should earnestly contend for the faith which was once delivered unto the saints. (KJV)

<u>Jude 14</u>: And Enoch also, the seventh from Adam, prophesied of these, saying, Behold, the Lord cometh with ten thousands of his saints. (KJV)

<u>John 14:6</u>: Jesus saith unto him, I am the way, the truth, and the life; no man cometh unto the Father, but by me. (KJV)

<u>I Corinthians 6:2</u>: Do ye not know that the saints will judge the world? and if the world shall be judged by you, are ye unworthy to judge the smallest matters? (KJV)

<u>Revelation 17:6</u>: And I saw the woman drunken with the blood

of the saints, and with the blood of the martyrs of Jesus; and when I saw her, I wondered with great admiration. (KJV)

Priests take situations of others and perform a sacrificial service; Saints receive direct communication from deities and deliver necessary information to those concerned. Not every person will be granted the ability to communicate with angels and deities.

Saints are people who have a genetic code in their blood for a personal hotline to the Angelic chambers. Communication skills must be matured; can be lost (by ignoring or ignorance) or weakened, and must be strengthened, or exercised. As the communication skills are strengthened and the measure of intensity rises, a Saint title can be achieved. God decides. God is the only source who can measure the level of strength in the communication skill.

In Jude 3, "once delivered" denotes a Spirit of "saint" that once existed in the bloodline will come again. One time, somewhere in the bloodline, the code for Saint was imparted. Notice in Jude 14 the reference to a specific generation, which foretold that the Saints would come when the Lord comes (returns). I'm going to suggest the reference to Enoch, the seventh from Adam, can connect to either Jacob's seventh son, Gad meaning: *exposing something valuable; to cut or furrow to expose treasure, fortune*; or to solely Enoch, which means: *discernment; wisdom or sustaining insight in the Laws of the Creator.*

There is a specific reason for the mention of being the seventh (generation) from Adam. Gad and Enoch provide a perfect description for a Saint.

The Saints will become evident when the Ancient Customs and Ways return. As the Ancient Customs and Ways are brought to light, they will assist in the resurrection of what is referenced as Jesus. The destruction of the Ancient Customs and Ways is equivalent to Jesus being put in the tomb. Because of the strength and involvement of the Angel(s), the stone is rolled away and the Ancient Ways will be resurrected. The Ancient Customs and Ways have not been here; The Way of Jesus has not been here, which tells me, the Saints haven't been here either.

<u>Threads</u>: Israel; Mysteries; People Groups

SALVATION

Salvation: Rescue; deliverance from destruction.

Revelation 12:10: And I heard a loud voice saying in heaven, Now is come salvation, and strength, and the kingdom of our God and the power of his Christ: for the accuser of our brethren is cast down, which accused them before our God day and night. (KJV)

I Peter 1:13: Wherefore, gird up the loins of your mind, be sober and hope to the end for the grace that is to be brought unto you at the revelation of Jesus Christ. (KJV)

The revelation, or realization of whatever all needs to be brought to our attention, does not arrive until "the end" of a season (of some event); "to be brought" references a future event. That future event includes now, 2022, not 500 or 2,000 years ago. Previous definitions and descriptions given for Salvation can be tossed aside.

What would humans be rescued from? The People Group that has the *Heaven Energy* code in their blood have been lost and wandering in the wilderness, totally clueless about their assignment and how they are to help others. Those people must come to the knowledge of many details (of the lost customs) that will bring forth an element of rescue for them and others. Since Jesus represents Natural Healthcare, the rescue would encompass health issues.

When a person comes to the realization of something they take an action. Example: You realize your cholesterol is too high; you take action to bring it down. There must be an action on the part of the assigned People Group and those who need their help. The Healthcare attached to the assigned People Group has been non-existent for hundreds of years, causing the health of mankind everywhere to gradually decline. A new diagnosis comes out every year and that alone should give clear indication that humanity is moving in the wrong direction. This is the cycle that needs to come to an end. To sit and hope and do nothing will get you nowhere other than into a more difficult situation. The assigned People Group needs to take action and get in position to avoid their demise as well. Action brings forth reaction, a manifestation. Humanity can/will be rescued from decaying, suffering, diseased physical bodies!

Will humans still die? Yes, the Spirit will vacate the physical body but it would not be due to decay, disease or decline. Exiting the physical body is to be like taking a trip. Trip experience examples in Scripture are Moses (Deuteronomy 34) and Peter. Peter states in *II Peter 1:14* that he is delivering his final message to the people because he's been notified of his departure (decease); his physical body is going to give up the ghost.

The intended way for departing would be something like this: You receive a message from one of God's messengers that your departure date is in "X" number days/years; you are instructed to "get your affairs in order because the chariot will be by to pick you up" on that date. You continue your daily activities, making sure all things are in order and your ticket for departure comes up and you peacefully take your final breath. This is much better than what many humans have gone through in order to move on to their eternity. Suffering in ways that result in having to rely on others for help in daily activities cannot be a pleasant experience. No thank you!

Threads: Christ

SIN

<u>Sin</u>: One of the two forms of the 21st letters of the Hebrew alphabet; a transgression of a religious or moral law. Deliberate disobedience.

<u>Note</u>: One can be conceived in Sin, leaving the theory of Sin being solely a deliberate act as folly.

<u>Romans 3:23</u>: *For all have sinned, and come short of the glory of God. (KJV)*

<u>Psalm 51:5</u>: *Indeed, I was guilty when I was born; I was sinful when my mother conceived me. (HCS)*

<u>Numbers 14:18</u>: *The Lord is longsuffering, and of great mercy, forgiving iniquity and transgression, and by no means clearing the guilty, visiting the iniquity of the fathers (ancestors) upon the children unto the third and fourth generation. (Insert added) (KJV)*

<u>Romans 8:23</u>: *And not only that, but we ourselves who have the Spirit as the firstfruits, we also groan within ourselves, eagerly waiting for adoption, the redemption of our bodies. (HCS)*

<u>Isaiah 58:12</u>: *Your people will rebuild the ancient ruins and will raise up the age-old foundations; you will be called*

Repairer of Broken Walls, Restorer of Streets with Dwellings. (KJV)

1 John 1:7: But if we walk in the light, as he is in the light, we have fellowship one with another, and the blood of Jesus Christ his Son cleanseth us from all sin. (KJV)

Sin has been woven into the human body since Adam and Eve were removed from the Garden. Sin blocks the glory. Now, how do we go about getting rid of it? The process of elimination is a bit more complex than most have been taught, and has little to do with a prayer.

First, humans have inherited Sin, and self-inflicted Sin. Two categories. Sin is harmful frequencies in the blood cells created by lingering harmful E-motions. Let's suppose God's frequency is 999 Hz. Human blood was designed to carry that particular frequency throughout life. Due to varying circumstances, such as traumas, unaddressed E-motional situations, meditating on negative thoughts, verbal abuses, exposure to excessive electrical frequencies that would come from computers or cell phones, even power stations, the 999 Hz gets dialed down a notch every time an opposing frequency is encountered. Let's say in an average day a person encounters opposing frequencies that take the total blood cell frequencies down to 666 Hz. If PROPER steps are not taken to erase the opposing frequencies and allow the God frequency of 999 Hz space to return, after a period of time disease takes root. These frequencies, high or low, pass through the generational bloodline.

When unaddressed they continue down the genetic line and eventually result in multiple health issues. A gradual loss of electrical power within the body is a result. The inherited frequencies, which initiated in Great Grandpa as trauma from participating in war, trickles down the generational line and becomes cancer or heart disease or a number of other deadly situations. In addition, those imprints of trauma frequencies that Great Grandpa had can play out as anxiety in the recipient three generations later.

When Sin frequencies are floating around in your bloodstream, which came from various personal experiences or experiences of ancestors, it is considered darkness or even "death" in Scripture. Everyone has them. Your life to this point has been a combination of several sets of grandparents' *E-motional* traumas, experiences, fixated thoughts, opinions, and so on. Fluid/water records electricity. (*See study of Dr. Masaru Emoto of Japan on how electrical currents and human thoughts change the particles in water*). Those Sin frequencies actually create sound. To my knowledge, there has not been a recording made of the sounds that come from human blood, other than the sound created by the movement of the blood. Sounds from outer space and below the surface of the ocean are recordable, why not blood sounds? This brings rise to the thought of development of a way to record the sound frequencies of blood to determine the spiritual status.

What is in the blood plays out in the mind, which then leads to symptoms of whatever the ancestor experienced. Think of it like this, the blood is the DVD; the brain is the TV screen on which the DVD projects. Clean blood would have a harmonious sound; it would move life through the body (versus death and decay). It means the individual would not be experiencing the ancestor *E-motions* and previously recorded experiences any longer. It opens opportunity to be "you."

Adam and Eve did not have the blood frequency depletion until a spiritual (electrical, *E-motion*) influence led them in the wrong direction. This tells me there is a way to erase the harmful frequencies. God created us without disease so there is a way to reverse things and get back to disease free.

Our bodies contain electrical currents; electrical currents assist in repair of the harmful frequencies. Electrical highways of the body are called Meridians; electrical centers are called Wheels in Ezekiel.

Scripture references the Ancient Ruins or the Ancient Past. There are Customs and dietary guidelines that were lost through time that not only assist in elimination of the echoes of our ancestors, but with the day-to-day function of the internal systems, organs and glands.

Iniquities and transgressions produce their own level of damage to the body. While sin falls under a category of breaking a moral law or acting out an offense, error or fault, an Iniquity is an immoral act that continues without repentance or a premeditated choice of such acts; to be crooked, perverse or have an evil regard to the things that are upright. Transgressions are a violation that pushes beyond the limits; to cast off God's authority; rebellious.

Translations of Scripture can often use the word "sin" in cases where the subject references transgression or iniquity. Remember, Sin is what is recorded in the blood cells (and 'testifies against us', Isaiah 59:12); Iniquities are of one's own doing. Transgressions are the acts that took place in the past that developed a way of living that falls outside of God's design. While the acts that initiated the change of how life is lived and society functions most likely were not of your doing, how you live your life amongst all the cultural or social "norms" (ethics, morals, diet, exercise, healthcare) is your responsibility.

The ability to gain the level of health and vitality that avoids and casts off any disease or harmful decay of the physical functions of the body not only requires a person to address the sin(s) issues, they must also identify and change the Iniquity(ies) and Transgression(s). These may be a little harder to identify given the gradual progression toward destruction society, cultures and moral acceptances have led us. Transgressions have become woven into the tapestry of acceptable patterns.

Numbers 5:31: The husband will be free of guilt, but the woman will bear the consequences of her guilt. (HCS)

In the verse above, woman references the spirit (electricity or energy) activity that takes place within the physical body structure. A simple example of what may be experienced would be your physical energy runs out easily; you feel tired or fatigued. The husband (physical) is a connection to the Christ transformation process of erasing the Sins from the blood cells, the status we are to long for. The Christ transformation process does not take away the guilt of an Iniquity or Transgression. (See Topic: Bride/Groom). Being of male gender does not get you off the hook when it comes to paying a price for any guilty sentence imposed.

An Iniquity does not pass down through the generations according to Ezekiel 18:20. In the situation of Iniquity, you get to pay your own invoice. (See also, Ezekiel 28:18 and 44:12)

Psalm 32:5: Then I acknowledged my sin to You and did not conceal my iniquity. I said, I will confess my transgressions to the Lord, and You took away the guilt of my sin. (HCS)

Transgressions arise out of participation in what most people today would categorize as a social norm; or how life is 'done'; or how/what things are accepted, or not. It's the cultural accepted norms that human powers and opinions have built. Believe it or not, many of the "norms" we identify with today can walk a person directly into a life of Transgression. These "norms" were developed out of what is called Jacob's rebellion described in Micah 1. Things became turned upside down over a long period of time all because of the decisions and actions of a specific group of people. (Refer to: VI. A Glance at History).

Galatians 3:19: Why then was the law given? It was added because of transgressions until the Seed to whom the promise is made would come. The law was put into effect through angels by means of a mediator. (HCS)

The law spoken of is the laws that govern nature, the natural cycles that many witness each year in the form of seasons. Those laws of nature apply to the interior function required to keep the physical body functioning. Those laws govern the physical body until the "Seed" (Specific People Group) has come and the Spirit (unseen force or electricity) takes over the function of the body. Just like the production of electrical vehicles, so will become our physical body.

Thread: Blood

SOLOMON

<u>Solomon</u>: To become whole or complete; righteous recompense; peace offering, reward. [Arabim-publications.com]

I Corinthians 6:19: What? Know ye not that your body is the temple of the Holy Ghost which is in you, which ye have of God, and ye are not your own? (KJV)

Solomon, King David's son, was assigned to build the Temple. Jesus, David and Solomon were from the Judah bloodline. The physical body is a Temple for God, not a structure of stone and wood built by hands.

This verse is directed to the people who have successfully completed the protocols to qualify for Holy Ghost accompaniment. The meaning of Solomon as described above and in I Kings 5:12 when the Lord gave Solomon wisdom, tells how the physical body is prepared as a Temple for the inhabitance of Holy Ghost. There is a preparation (building) process that takes place in and through the body first. The Holy Ghost doesn't reside just anywhere. The frame is the physical body and the interior needs proper remodeling and function. There are qualifications to be met such as righteousness and wisdom that develop through a Christ transformation. It takes effort to build or remodel a house and wisdom to know what tools (nutrition, diet, etc.) to use is necessary. Healthy function of the body is required. Foods that are common in the standard American diet can interfere with the ability to house the Holy Ghost. The Ancient Wisdom must be recovered before proper Temples can be constructed that qualify to house the Holy Ghost.

Threads: Israel, People Groups

SON OF MAN OR SON OF GOD

<u>Mark 14:21</u>: *The Son of man indeed goeth, as it is written of him; but woe to that man by whom the Son of man is betrayed! Good were it for that man if he had never been born. (*Note: man/he can represent social or government structures in the world, not necessarily a particular person.) (KJV)*

A Son of Man is an individual who leans toward a material answer or is focused on the world's approach and opinion; one whose physical body operates solely by fleshly means. Such as, education, healthcare, religion, lifestyle, and so on. Son of Man is also a reference to an event unfolding in the physical realm. Son of God is an individual who has escaped the pressures of society driven by mankind, has gone through the Christ suffering transformation and lives free of external influences. Son of God is also a reference to an event that takes place in the unseen realm; the cells in the body are now dominated by Spirit energy/light. To achieve a Son of God status (the ability and authority to cause change in the unseen realm), suffering and sacrifices, possibly even unto near death, is required. (Consider the story of Job; or the Myth of the Phoenix/Firebird, who rises up from mere ashes.) Natural healing of the body escorts the individual to the Son of God status. Knowing how and what to do to make your way through the suffering/sacrifice journey is important. Throwing up the hands and ignoring symptoms can result in an act of suicide.

In today's society an automatic response to a form of disturbance in the body is to seek medical aid to relieve the pain and suffering. Making your way through the Valley of the Shadow of Death was easier to navigate in the Ancient Days due to their knowledge in use of herbs, essential oils, and food. In general, one can assume those who lived in the Ancient Ways were a little tougher than most today. Although Natural remedies are more prevalent today than just 20 years ago, society still lacks many components to the Natural Healthcare and Wellness lifestyle.

Certainly, symptoms in the body need to be addressed and one should seek out a means to uncover the root of a symptom. How one chooses to address the symptom will determine how much or how long the Christ transformation process may take. Again, it is not wise to do nothing and ignore a symptom. There is a process to learning how to read a symptom and knowing how to treat it. It takes many years and a lot of experience to achieve a skill in interpreting what the body is attempting to tell you through a symptom. Society has grown accustom to asking medical professionals instead of interpreting the messages their body is presenting themselves. There is no one size fits all when it comes to Natural Healthcare but there are some general applications that assist or direct the physical body in recovery.

Success in the journey of suffering and sacrifice earns the Son of God title. Before the suffering, an individual is a Son of Man.

Thread: Dead

SOUL

<u>Soul</u>: A part of humans regarded as immaterial, immortal, separable from the body at death, capable of moral judgment and susceptible to happiness or misery in a future state. The part of a human when disembodied after death.

<u>Soul</u> (author's definition): The Soul expresses the song produced by the frequencies in the blood. The "Wow, I feel great today" and the "Oh, I don't feel so well today."

<u>Hell</u> (author's definition): Troublesome experiences whether physically or emotionally; turmoil on the interior of the body. Personal, miserable experiences that linger or remain regardless of efforts to escape their grasp.

<u>Genesis 2:7</u>: *And the Lord God formed man of the dust of the ground, and breathed into his nostrils the breath of life; and the man became a living soul. (KJV)*

<u>Psalm 116: 3-4</u>: *The sorrows of death compassed me, the pains of hell gat hold upon me; I found trouble and sorrow. Then called I upon the name of the Lord; O Lord, I beseech thee, deliver my soul. (KJV)*

Psalm 116:7-8: Return unto they rest, O my soul; for the Lord hath dealt bountifully with thee. For though has delivered my soul from death, mine eyes from tears and my feet from falling. (KJV)

There are several Scriptures describing Soul and most speak of the evidence of an *E-motion*. Actions or an environment in general can result in a joyful Soul or a miserable Soul; a Soul filled with life or a Soul bound for death. The lack of hope, interest or ability is described as dead. Word play is common in Scripture and requires a dash of common sense at times.

Breath ignites the spark for a living Soul. The act of proper breathing must be a component of keeping the Soul alive, assisting in wiping away the *E-motional* imprints. Ever heard the expression "Just Breathe" after encountering a stressful event? It can also be established that since there is a living Soul, there must also be a dead Soul. Death of the Soul can take place while the physical body is fully functioning and alive. A good example is described in Psalm 23. This raises questions about whether the Soul continues at death for transition to a new location.

Sorrow and trouble result in a weary, "hell" experience for the Soul. An act of connection to a greater power (Lord references a higher authority) will set the Soul free from the sorrow and trouble. Many have experienced a setback during loss of a loved one; a time where the body is simply drained of its energy. This is a time when the forces of *E-motions* have flooded the body draining the Soul of its "Alive"-ness. The Soul will be lifted up when sorrow and trouble are removed. Sounds easy enough, right?

The Soul is described as having experiences of ups and downs, an ongoing form of shift or change. *Example*:

Many individuals who suffer a level of depression or mental illness did not think their way into that state of existence. They may have gone through a situation that contributed to their condition but it is unlikely they alone developed the condition. It is an accumulation of sorrowful, troublesome experiences that result in an individual being locked into a seemingly inescapable state of existence. It was not their choice. Therapies will not cure these types of depression or mental illness yet Scripture describes the ability to go from a state of sorrow to an uplifted, resurrected state. Sticking with the examples of depression and mental illness that often are inherited, a clear explanation is the frequency in the blood that has produced what is labeled today as depression or mental illness. To change the status of the Soul, the blood frequencies that equate to sorrow, and so on, must be erased.

Visual: A child tragically experiences the loss of his/her parents through some act of violence, witnessed by the child. This experience remains unaddressed, tucked away in the recesses of the mind because of the fear and anxiety.

The child grows up and has a family. The son/daughter born into this new family develops signs of mental health issues. No apparent reason for the development of the mental health issues; typical school stress or childhood playmate stress but no glaring events. The imprint of trauma from the parent to the son/daughter continues on down the generational lines. This passing along of trauma is what Scripture calls Sin (of the fathers). The result of the fear and anxiety imprint that is manifest by the current recipient is the activity of what is called the Soul. The Soul is not what would go to a literal Heaven or Hell at death; the Soul is what conducts the actual playback as a result of the type of frequencies in the blood. The Soul can either reside in a state of Heaven(ly) bliss or it can reside in a state of Hell(ish) situations. Erasing the harmful blood imprints to release the individual from the merry-go-round of sorrow and trouble is a key.

The status of the frequencies in the blood is what Scripture labels the Soul. To avoid lengthy details and from lack of a more appropriate descriptions, the term Soul was applied.

Threads: Bread of Life; Breath

VIRGIN MARY

Luke 1:26-31: *And in the sixth month the angel Gabriel was sent from God unto a city of Galilee, named Nazareth, to a virgin espoused to a man whose name was Joseph, of the house of David; and the virgin's name was Mary. And the angel came in unto her and said, "Hail, thou that are highly favored, the Lord is with thee, blessed are thou among women." And when she saw him, she was troubled at his saying, and cast in her mind what manner of salutation this should be. And the angel said unto her, Fear not, Mary; for thou has found favor with God. And behold, thou shalt conceive in thy womb, and bring forth a son, and shalt call his name Jesus. (KJV)*

Mary represents the bloodline that carries the gifts connected to Natural Healthcare. She had the genetic code that produces a Natural healing. She was joined to the "I AM." Mary had a connection that is referenced by the description of being "highly favored." How did Mary achieve being highly favored? The genetic code of a Spiritual Gift of healing developed in Mary and was then shared with and extended to others. The role of Jesus is the Natural Healthcare and Wellness that was brought forth. Mary had the revelation and took steps to achieve the Natural Healthcare and Wellness in the body. Jesus was assigned to live it out as an example for those with the genetic code to know how to activate their Gift of healing and how to extend that healing power to others to assist in their recovery.

Gabriel gave Mary a heads-up about the genetic imprint in her blood. Why? The Spiritual Gift of Natural Healthcare and Wellness can lay dormant, unknown to the owner of it and to those they encounter. Some interior modifications to the body need to be made before the Gift can fully develop and become evident.

Applying a little bit of Biology to this story changes the interpretation that the world identifies. It takes the joining of cells, sperm and egg, to develop a fetus. Female physical bodies do not contain the two components necessary to produce a physical baby and providing an elevated form of electrical power does not result in a sperm cell. (And all the women said, "thank the Lord!") I propose that this particular story is referencing the manifestation of a Gift that is lived out through a lifestyle of Natural Healthcare and Wellness. This interpretation does not eliminate the fact that Jesus walked the Earth as a human.

Threads: Bride; Israel; People Groups

VOW and OATH

Vow: A solemn or earnest pledge or promise binding the person making it to perform a specified act or behave in a certain way; marriage vows.

Oath: A solemn, formal declaration or promise to fulfill a pledge, often calling on God, a god, or a sacred object as witness; the words or formula of such a declaration or promise.

*Matthew 5:33-37: Again you have heard that it was said to our ancestors, You must not break your oath, but you must **keep your oaths to the Lord**. But I tell you, **don't take an oath at all**: either by heaven, because it is God's throne; or by the earth, because it is His footstool; or by Jerusalem, because it is the city of the great King. Neither should you swear by your head, because you cannot make a single hair white or black. But let your word "yes" be "yes" and your "no" be "no"; anything more than this is from the evil one. (Emphasis Added) (KJV)*

Ecclesiastes 5:5: Better that you do not vow than that you vow and not fulfill it. (HCS)

II Corinthians 11:2: For I am jealous over you with godly jealousy; for I have espoused you to one husband, that I may present you as a chaste virgin to Christ. (KJV)

For Jesus to be so direct in His instruction in Matthew could indicate there is an element of joining one person to another (person, career or what have you) through a vow or oath that would cause interference. A vow directs dedication and service to the one the vow or oath is shared with.

Could a vow hinder the ability to be a "Bride of Christ"? There is a "without stain or wrinkle" notation (*Ephesians 5:27*) that goes along with qualifying for a Bride status. The stain would reference removal of the Sin frequencies. *E-motional* connections can result in a bond or commitment, which leads one to think that an *E-motional* connection to your job or to another person can be an obstacle preventing the ability for becoming a Bride. Job 16:8 references wrinkles as a result of the Soul wounds and decay his body was experiencing, those Soul wounds were *E-motions*.

Thread: Adultery

WHEELS

<u>Wheel</u>: A solid disk or a rigid circular ring connected by spokes to a hub, designed to turn around an axle passed through the center. A steering device on a vehicle.

<u>Chakra</u>: Any of the points in the human body described in yogic philosophy as centers of vital energy, especially one of seven such centers that are aligned with the spinal column. Sanskrit for Wheel.

<u>Cunning</u>: Crafty in the use of special resources. Care; Design.

<u>Ezekiel 10:9-10, 15-17</u>: And when I looked, behold the four wheels by the cherubims, one wheel by one cherub and another wheel by another cherub; and the appearance of the wheels was as the colour of a beryl stone. And as for their appearances, the four had one likeness, as if a wheel had been in the midst of a wheel. <u>v. 15-17</u>: And the cherubims were lifted up. This is the living creature that I saw by the river of Chebar. (Chebar: great, mighty or much; already established). And when the cherubims went, the wheels went by them; and when the cherubims lifted up their wings to mount up from the earth, the same wheels also turned not from beside them. When they stood, these stood; and when they were lifted up, these lifted up themselves also: for the spirit of the living creature was in them. (KJV)

I Samuel 16:14-16: But the Spirit of the Lord departed from Saul, and an evil spirit from the Lord troubled him. And Saul's servants said unto him, Behold now, an evil spirit from God troubleth thee. Let our lord now command thy servants, which are before thee, to seek out a man, who is a cunning player on an harp; and it shall come to pass, when the evil spirit from God is upon thee, that he shall play with his hand and thou shall be well. (KJV)

Ezekiel 1:22: And the likeness of the firmament upon the heads of the living creature was as the color of the terrible crystal, stretch forth over their heads above. (KJV)

Ezekiel 1:24: And when they went, I heard the noise of their wings, like the noise of great waters, as the voice of the Almighty, the voice of speech, as the noise of an host; when they stood, they let down their wings. (KJV)

Ecclesiates 12:6: Before the silver cord is snapped, and the gold bowl is broken, and the jar is shattered at the spring, and the wheel is broken into the well; and the dust returns to the earth as it once was, and the Spirit returns to God who gave it. (KJV)

The Wheels described as living creatures by Ezekiel are electrical energy centers positioned along the spine. Ezekiel is describing what takes place when these Wheels are nurtured, or fully charged. The Wheels are like small batteries. They must be charged up; they can run down and can completely lose their charge. Various things cause a loss of charge, such as: neglect of re-charge; sickness; exposure to electronic devices that deplete or cause friction to the Wheel; stress, poor nutrition or extended periods of *E-motional* disturbance. These

Wheels must be nurtured in order for the physical body to remain healthy and organs to function properly.

Wheel imbalance or energy depletion could be the reference to the evil spirit from God in 1 Samuel and without a doubt there was some *E-motional* disturbance going on. When David played the harp, which is a symbol of Ireland and would connect to an Ancient Custom from Ireland, the evil spirit left and the Soul was uplifted.

Physical movements will cause Wheels to move. Wheels give off color when in motion, identified as amber, beryl, crystal, burnished brass. The colors described are also mineral stones; rocks used in various therapies or worn as support in the form of jewelry. Mineral stones are what a Priest's Ephod contained and what adorns the Bride for the Bridegroom. When the Wheels are working correctly and have ample velocity, you become a candidate for being a Bride. Mineral stones are mentioned in various verses and reference an element of Natural support, comfort, and so on.

Considering Ezekiel 1:22, there appears to be an element of contact with Heaven that takes place at the Crown Wheel on the top of the head. For a mental picture, think of the photos seen of Jesus with the glow around the top of His head.

Verse 24 speaks of a movement (they went) and noise. Noise is evidence of a vibration or activity. Waters represent *E-motions*, or acts of cleansing. Ezekiel is describing the Wheels in the physical body causing the fluids within the body, such as in the lymph system or kidneys and bladder, to move. Having a properly functioning waterway within the body is crucial for good health. Properly functioning and charged Wheels assist the body to eliminate toxins.

Ecclesiates 12:6 is talking about the process of the Wheels shutting down and the physical body turning off after the Spirit that the body housed has already left. Spirit goes first, then the physical function of the body. Lingering *E-motional* disturbances or inherited *E-motions* from ancestors that are recorded in the blood will hinder or shut down a Wheel's activity resulting in disease. God decides when the Spirit departs so if your Wheels begin shutting down prior to the date God has set for your Spirit to depart, you will struggle with disease, slowly advancing toward decay. Ecclesiates clears up many questions about what happens at the time of death.

Thread: Priest

WHITE HORSE

Horse: Power.

*Note: He and him (male) reference physical body not necessarily male.

Sat: symbol of an official position/status.

Crown (Wheel): is a sign of an ability to connect to Heaven Energy.

"Dipped in blood" has to do with genetic imprints that influence life.

"Eyes a flame of fire" speaks of blue eyes. Eyes are not yellow or orange leaving blue as the reference here.

Thigh signifies oath. God made an Oath (or Promise) to a specific People Group.

Genesis 12:11: And it came to pass, when he was come near to enter into Egypt, that he said unto Sarai his wife, Behold now, I know that thou art a fair woman to look upon. (KJV)

I Kings 1:3: So they sought for a fair damsel throughout all the coasts of Israel and found Abishag a Shunammite, and brought her to the king. (KJV)

<u>Song of Solomon 6:10</u>: Who is she that looketh forth as the morning, fair as the moon, clear as the sun, and terrible as an army with banners? (KJV)

<u>II Samuel 14:27</u>: And unto Absalom there were born three sons, and one daughter, whose name was Tamar: she was a woman of a fair countenance. (KJV)

<u>Revelation 6:2</u>: And I saw, and behold a white horse; and he that sat on him had a bow; and a crown was given unto him; and he went forth conquering, and to conquer. (KJV)

<u>Revelation 19:11-13, 16</u>: And I saw heaven opened, and behold a white horse; and he that sat upon him was called Faithful and True and in righteousness he doth judge and make war. His eyes were as a flame of fire, and on his head were many crowns; and he had a name written, that no man knew, but he himself. And he was clothed with a vesture dipped in blood; and his name is called The Word of God. <u>v. 16</u>: And he hath on his vesture and on his thigh a name written, KING OF KINGS, AND LORD OF LORDS. (KJV)

The verses above conclude a woman with fair complexion was often sought after. Women represent not only physically a female but can also be a Spirit that would come from such a woman. There is a power within that particular Spirit that comes from a woman with a fair complexion.

Through the ages the vision of Jesus riding on the White Horse descending down through the clouds is just that, a visual. The symbols referenced must be unraveled to understand what the true message is. There will not be a literal, physical human come through the clouds. Such an event defies the laws of gravity without a parachute. Jesus does represent a power that comes through Natural Healthcare that is returning. This Natural Healthcare is not here yet. It is what will return through the resurrection of Ancient Customs. The descriptions hidden within the verses point our attention to the class of Spiritual Royals, who have a fair complexion, blue eyes, and a genetic imprint that supports connecting to the *Heaven Energy*, who will by means of the invisible forces that reside in the sky/clouds, usher in the return of the Ancient Customs of Natural Healthcare. The preferred color of a horse for Royals is white.

Threads: Ancient Ways; Christ; Mysteries

See also, History of Uffington White Horse, Oxfordshire, England.

CONCLUSION

<u>Ezekiel 2:3-5, 9</u>: *And he said unto me, Son of man, I send thee to the children of Israel, to a rebellious nation that hath rebelled against me; they and their fathers have transgressed against me, even unto this very day. For they are impudent children and stiffhearted, I do send thee unto them; and thou shalt say until them, Thus saith the Lord God. And they, whether they will hear, or whether they will forbear, for they are a rebellious house, yet shall know that there hath been a prophet among them.* <u>v. 9</u>: *And when I looked, behold, an hand was sent unto me, and lo, a roll of a book was therein.*

RESOURCES

A&E Documentaries
Arabim-publications.com
Celtic Mythology by Philip Freeman
Cornish Witchcraft by the Estate of William H. Paynter
her.york.gov.uk
History Channel
Holy Bible, KJV and Holman Christian Standard
Merriam-Webster Dictionary and Thesaurus
Smithsonian Channel and Website

TRUSTING AND BELIEVING
HAVE BEEN CONTAMINATED
BY THE DESIRE TO UNDERSTAND

www.ingramcontent.com/pod-product-compliance
Lightning Source LLC
Chambersburg PA
CBHW030113240426
43673CB00002B/69